ORIGINAL JOURNALS

OF THE

LEWIS AND CLARK EXPEDITION

1804-1806

WITH FACSIMILES, MAPS, PLANS, VIEWS, PORTRAITS, AND A BIBLIOGRAPHY

ATLAS

*Of this Edition on Van Gelder Hand-made Paper
two hundred copies only have been printed
of which this is*

No.

ATLAS

ACCOMPANYING THE

ORIGINAL JOURNALS

OF THE

LEWIS AND CLARK EXPEDITION

1804-1806

BEING FACSIMILE REPRODUCTIONS OF MAPS, chiefly by William Clark, illustrating the route of the expedition, with sites of camping places and Indian villages, besides much miscellaneous data   Now for the first time published, from the original manuscripts in the possession of Mrs Julia Clark Voorhis and Miss Eleanor Glasgow Voorhis, together with a modern map of the route prepared especially for this volume

Edited, with Introduction, by

REUBEN GOLD THWAITES, LL.D.

Editor of " The Jesuit Relations and Allied Documents," etc

VOLUME EIGHT

NEW YORK

DODD, MEAD & COMPANY

1905

THE UNIVERSITY PRESS
CAMBRIDGE, U S A

Original Journals of the
Lewis & Clark Expedition

Edited, with Introduction, Notes, and Index by
Reuben Gold Thwaites

As Published in 1904

Volume VIII, Atlas

Vol. VIII, Atlas Trade Paperback ISBN: 1-58218-659-6
Vol. VIII, Atlas Hardcover ISBN: 1-58218-668-5

Digital Scanning and Publishing is a leader in the electronic republication of historical books and documents. We publish many of our titles as eBooks, as well as traditional hardcover and trade paper editions. DSI is commited to bringing many traditional and little known books back to life, retaining the look and feel of the original work.

©2001 DSI Digital Reproduction
First DSI Printing: February 2001

Published by DIGITAL SCANNING, INC.
Scituate, MA 02066
www.digitalscanning.com

Original Journals of the Lewis and Clark Expedition
Four Photographs supplied with permission by
Ernst Mayr Library of the Museum of Comparative Zoology
Harvard University, Cambridge, MA 02138
"Snags On the Missouri River" (Vol. 1 part 1)
"Winter Village of the Minatarres" Vol. 1 Part II)
"Fort Mackenzie" (Vol. II Part 1)
"Indians Hunting the Bison" (Vol. III, Part 1)

INTRODUCTION

THE remarkable series of charts given in this volume illustrate in detail almost the entire route of the Lewis and Clark expedition, both on the outward and the return journeys, with sites of camping-places and Indian villages, and further enriched with much interesting comment on the country and the natives. An account of their discovery will be found in the Introduction to Vol. I of the present series, pp. l–liii Save for Nos. 1–3, which are copies of contemporary French and Spanish manuscript maps, and doubtless were carried upon the expedition, several traced from rude Indian drawings, and No. 37, which bears Lewis's chirography, all appear to have been the work of Clark, who was the recognized draughtsman of the party. When we consider the conditions under which these charts were drawn, — in the field, with crude astronomical instruments, and information derivable chiefly from daily observation and Indian reports, — their relative accuracy and topographical comprehension are worthy of our highest praise; they are eloquent witnesses of Clark's undoubted engineering skill.

The charts fall readily into certain groups:

I. A preliminary series (Nos. 1–3) being tracings of contemporary French and Spanish manuscripts. In this series we may also include No. 4, showing the neighborhood of the first winter's camp in Illinois, at River Dubois, opposite the mouth of the Missouri.

II. But one map (No. 5) appears to be extant, of the lower Missouri — that for the stretch above St. Charles, across a large portion of the present State of Missouri. Others are missing either by accident or because this portion of the river was well known to French and Spanish fur-traders, who even

[v]

thus early made annual voyages as far as the present site of Omaha.

III. When the expedition entered the comparatively un- known region peopled by the fierce Sioux and Arikara tribes, a careful record of the river's course is shown in a series of small but exceedingly accurate maps (Nos. 6–11). These lay down the river channel continuously from a point near the southern boundary of South Dakota as far up as the site of Fort Mandan, some thirty-five miles above the present city of Bismarck — thus giving almost the entire stretch of the Missouri's course across the two Dakotas, with the islands, bends, and Indian villages upon the banks as they were found by the expedition a hundred years ago

IV. This group consists of Nos. 11–13, prepared at Fort Mandan on information received from French and British traders, as well as from native reports   No. 11 shows the trail from the Assiniboin region, over which the Northwest Com- pany's factors had come — to find, to their chagrin, that the Americans had established themselves among the Mandans, who were accounted the former's especial customers.   Nos 12 and 13 are conjectural maps of the country to the west, indi- cating the overland trail to the Yellowstone and the chief topographical features of the eastern slope of the Rocky Mountains.

V. No 14 is one of the principal maps of the series.   It represents the course of the Missouri from Fort Mandan as far as the Falls, and embraces the route of the summer's travel in 1805 — from the time the Mandans were left behind (April 7) to the date when the portage was completed and the river approached through the Gates of the Mountains (July 15)   This map was prepared by Clark with skilful care; it embodies the results of a series of preliminary field sketches (Nos. 15–25), draughted from day to day on rough sheets on which the "Courses and Distances" for each day's travel were also indicated.   Using these eleven maps as a basis, Clark gives us in No. 14 the natural features, the affluents, the character of the banks, and the camping-places both going and returning; all this data being presented upon a Mercator's projection of squares of latitude and longitude. It is interesting to note that not possessing sheets of paper of sufficient size to produce so large a map, he pasted together those of ordinary dimensions. This was done at such angles that the sinuous course of the river is graphically represented. Nos. 26 and 26*a* are sketches of the topography of the Falls of the Missouri, and supplement those already published in volume three of this work, which were found in the codices of the journals proper.

Four additional maps were needed to complete the water route to the head-springs of Jefferson River, where the canoes were finally abandoned. These (Nos. 27–29*a*) portray in like careful manner: the Missouri through the Rocky Mountains, the Three Forks of that river, and the course of the Jefferson from its junction with Madison and Gallatin rivers through Beaver Head Valley to its upper forks. This was the course over which the expedition painfully struggled (July 16–Aug. 20, 1805) from the Great Falls, until it was no longer possible to drag or pole the canoes through the shallowing stream.

VI. We now come to three large maps, of which the first (No. 30) is probably the most important of the entire series: for herein is portrayed the much-discussed and little-understood route over the range of mountains lying between the head-springs of the Missouri and the plains of the Kooskooskee (Clearwater), where the friendly Flatheads (Chopunnish) preserved the expedition from starvation. On sheets of paper pasted together in the same ingenious fashion as before, Clark has laid down the entire horseback tour from Shoshoni Cove to the banks of the Lemhi; the crossing to the Bitterroot Valley—not perfectly elucidated up to the present publication; the passage down the Bitterroot; the rendezvous at Traveller's Rest; and the mountainous trail to the west, along the ridge north of the middle fork of the Kooskooskee, including the courses of Hungry and Collins creeks (so difficult to identify);

[vii]

and finally, the emergence upon Weippe Prairie, the habitat of the hospitable Flatheads.

No. 31 shows the entire course of the Kooskooskee, its junction with Lewis (Snake) River, and the latter's bed as far as the Columbia, which is also given to the Umatilla, as well as some portion of its course above the junction of the Lewis. The point where the canoes were built is indicated, and the descent of the three rivers from October 17–19 is charted in much detail.

The third of the three large maps (No. 32) portrays all the lower stretch of the Columbia, from about the point where it becomes the boundary between the present States of Oregon and Washington, to its discharge into the Pacific, together with a part of the coast line of the latter. This is interesting not only for the detail and accuracy with which the river's course is traced, but as being probably our first chart of that great waterway above the tidal region.

There follow several small sketch maps (Nos. 33–36), showing details of the Columbia, evidently prepared only as preliminary to the making of No. 32. They have, however, an interest of their own, in marking certain camping-places and giving some other particulars not reproduced on the larger chart.

VII. Nos. 37–39 were those made at Fort Clatsop. No. 38 shows Clark's exploration of the coast when on his journey (Jan. 6–10, 1806) in search of the spoils of the stranded whale.

VIII. The next group of maps (Nos. 40–44) are all of Indian origin, and represent the information obtained on the return journey from the natives of the Western slope, in relation to tribal location, natural objects, and various mountain trails. It was upon the data thus gathered that the explorers based the bold conception of dividing the party, each section seeking not only increased geographical knowledge, but a more practicable passage than they had found on the outward journey, between Missouri and Columbia waters.

No. 43 is especially interesting in this connection. It maps several native trails over the great divide, and three available routes from Traveller's Rest to the Missouri — the most northerly of which was followed by Lewis, and the most southerly by Clark.

IX. The last group is devoted to Clark's return route. Of these, Nos. 45 and 46 refer to his crossing (July 4–9, 1806) from the Bitterroot Valley to the Forks of the Jefferson, and are somewhat contradictory and confused. A careful local study, however, may elucidate the main features of the trail, as well as throw light upon the outward journey between these two points.

Nos. 47 and 48 likewise indicate the journey from the Three Forks to the Yellowstone, over what is now the famous Bozeman Pass, and approximating the present route of the Northern Pacific Railway.

The remainder of the maps (Nos. 49–53) portray the basin of the Yellowstone. Here is the only gap in the continuity of the series. The first four maps are contiguous, and bring us to the neighborhood of old Fort Sarpy, near the eastern boundary of the present Crow Indian Reservation. One small map (No. 53) of the Yellowstone, near its junction with the Missouri, closes this series of original charts.

X. No. 54 has been prepared especially for this volume, on the basis of the maps above enumerated, and represents, on a condensed scale, the route of the entire journey in relation to modern conditions, from the mouth of the Missouri to the Pacific and return. Necessarily compressed in order to present a bird's-eye view of the whole, the details must be sought through a close study of Clark's originals, in connection with the text of the journals themselves.

The points of the compass are roughly indicated by the placing of the captions at the south side of the maps.

R. G. T.

LIST OF MAPS

[xi]

30. "From Jeffersons River to the Forks of Kooskooske over the Rocky Mountains from the 25th of August to the 9th of October 1805."

This map is of especial importance, as showing the route over the divide, heretofore in doubt.

Part I. From camp of August 24 on Jefferson River to camp of September 3 on Clark's River.

Part II From camp of September 4 on Clark's River to camp of September 16 on Kooskooskee River

Part III Kooskooskee River, from camp of September 17 to camp of October 7.

31. "Sketch of Kooskooske & Lewis's River from the 7th to the 19th of Oc.^{tr} 1805 "

Part I. Kooskooske and Lewis's Rivers, showing route from October 7 to just below camp of October 11.

Part II. Lewis's and upper Columbia Rivers, from camp of October 12 to that of October 19

32 "Sketch of the Columbia River from the forks, & the 19th of October 1805 to the 1st of Jany on the Pacific Ocean." The map also indicates camping places on the return journey, in April, 1806.

Part I. From camp of October 19 to that of October 29, showing the "Great Falls."

Part II. From Camp of October 29 just above the "Great Rapid" to camp of November 5

Part III From camp of November 5 to the Pacific, showing also the Pacific coast from "Cape Shalwater" on the north to Cape Lookout on the south.

33. Rapids of the Columbia; with camps of October 26–28, 1805.

34. The Columbia River from the Rapids to Wappato Island, showing camps of October 29 — November 4, 1805, and the return camp on March 30, 1806

35. A medley of sketches.

I. Pacific Coast, in neighborhood of Haley's Bay, and showing camps of November 8–17, 1805

II. Camp of November 7; detail.

III. Camp of November 8; detail.

IV. Lower reaches of Columbia, showing outward camps of November 4–6, 1805, and the return camps of March 27–29, 1806.

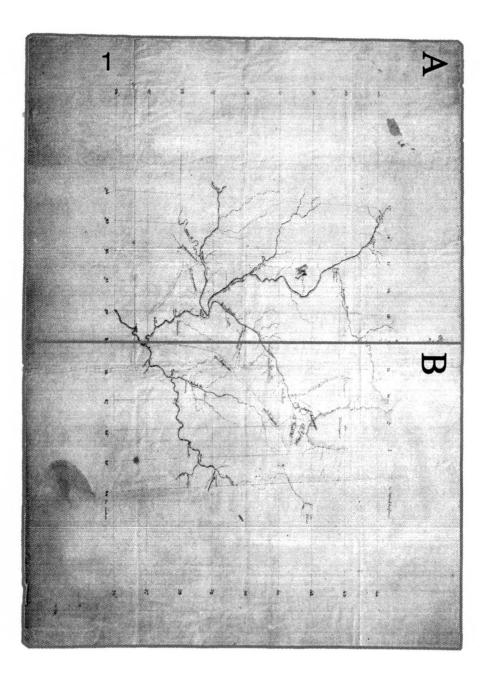

1.   The Upper Mississippi, Lower Ohio, and Lower Missouri rivers.
Evidently copied from a contemporary French manuscript map.

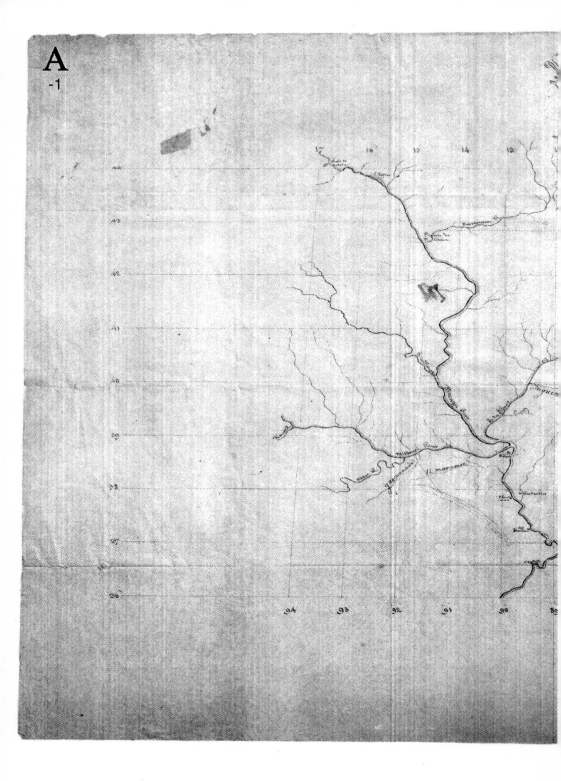

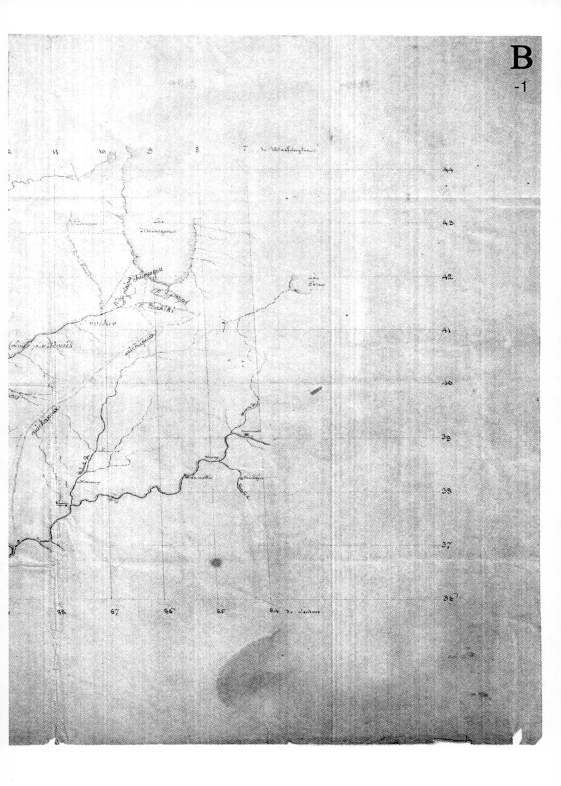

B
-1

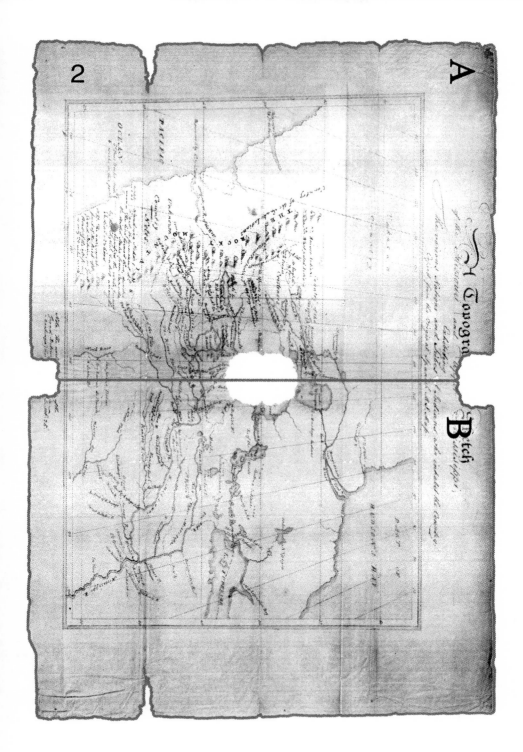

2. "A Topogr[aphical] Sketch of the Missouri and Upper Mississippi, exhibiting
The various Nations and Tribes of Indians who inhabit the Country.
Copied from the original Spanish MS. Map."

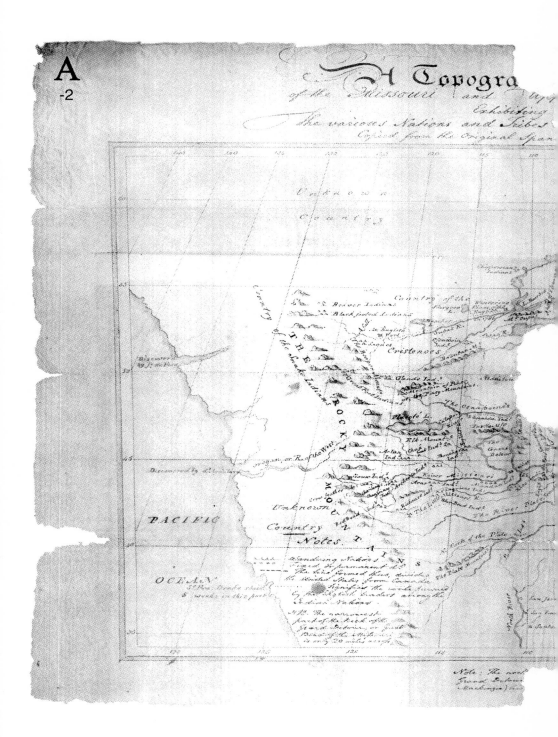

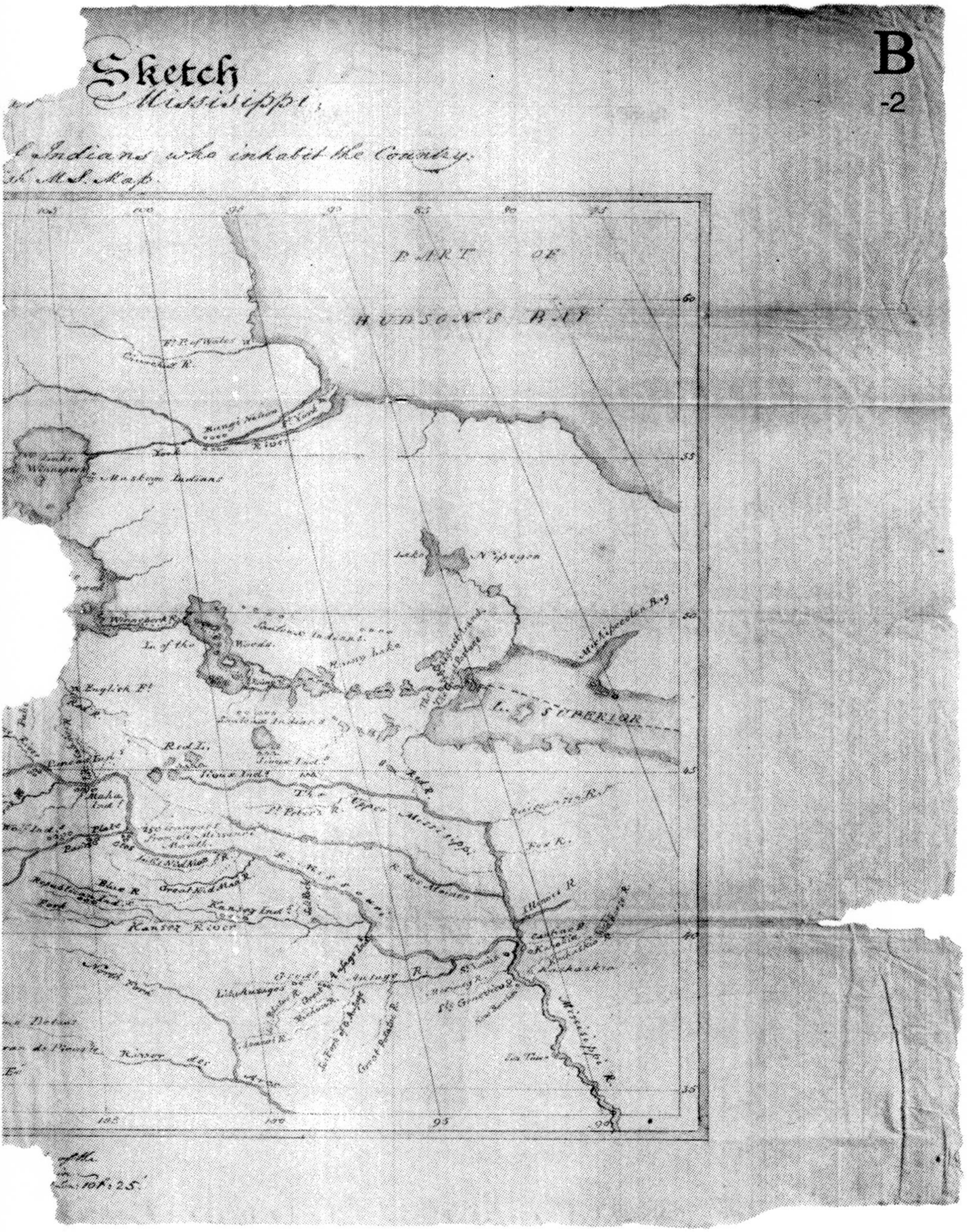

Sketch

Missisippi.

Indians who inhabit the Country.

MS. Map.

PART OF

HUDSON'S BAY

60

55

50

L. SUPERIOR

45

40

35

105   100   95   90   85   80   75

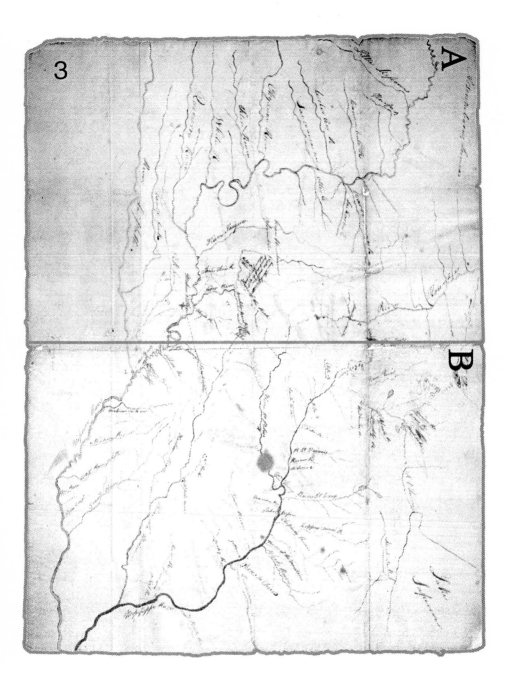

3. The Upper Mississippi system, and the Missouri system as far as the Mandans.

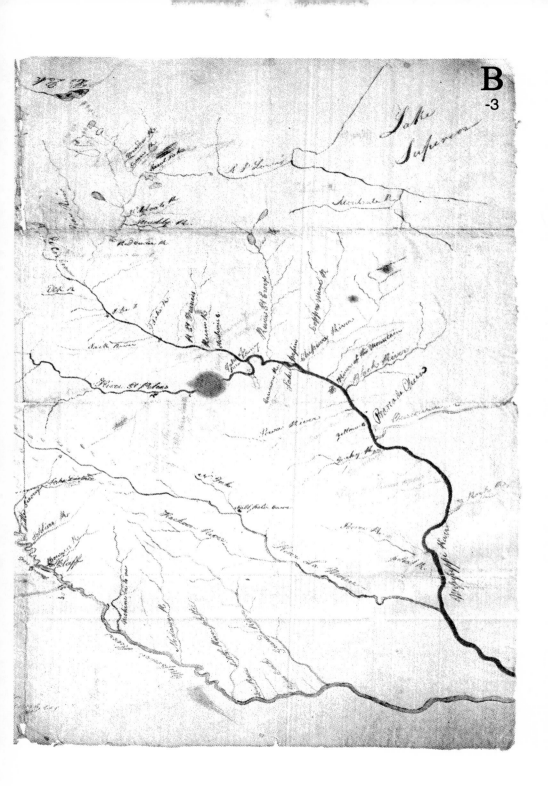

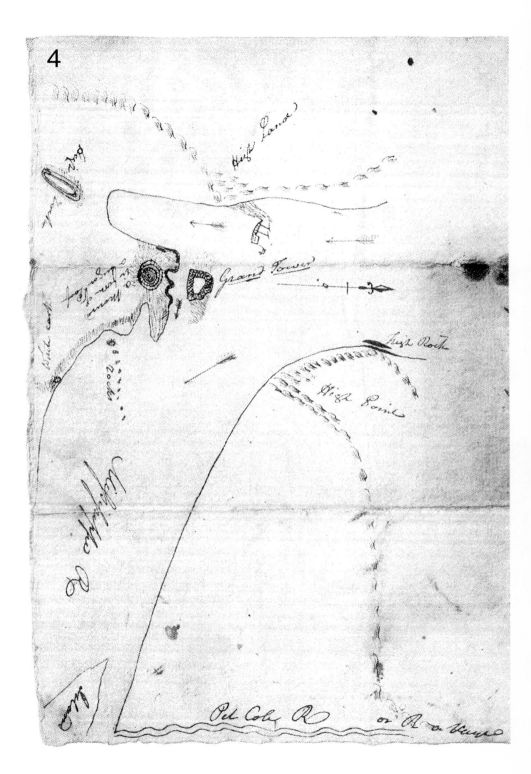

4. The neighborhood of Camp River Dubois, 1803-04.

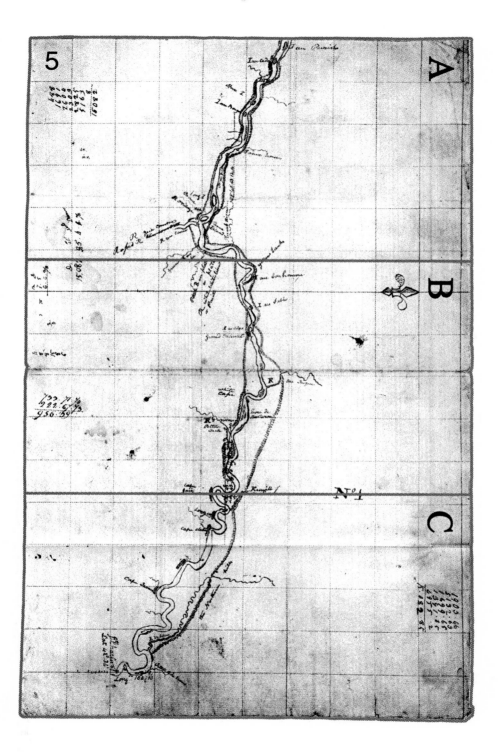

5. The Missouri River, from St. Charles to Isle au Parish.
Route from May 21-about June 20, 1804.

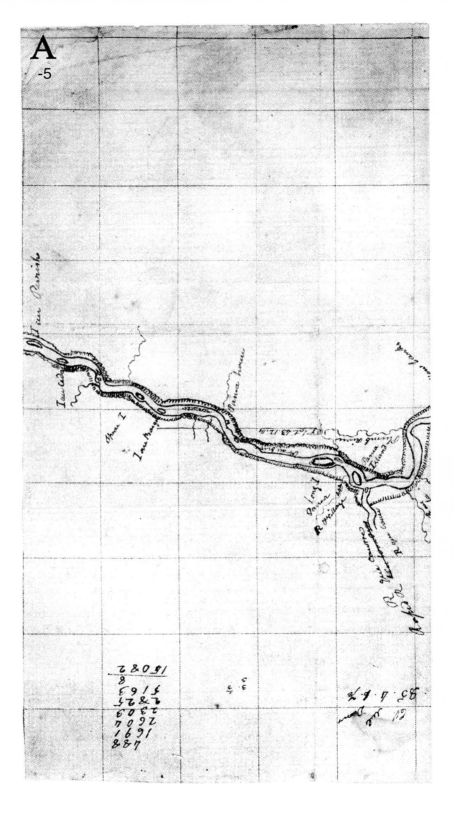

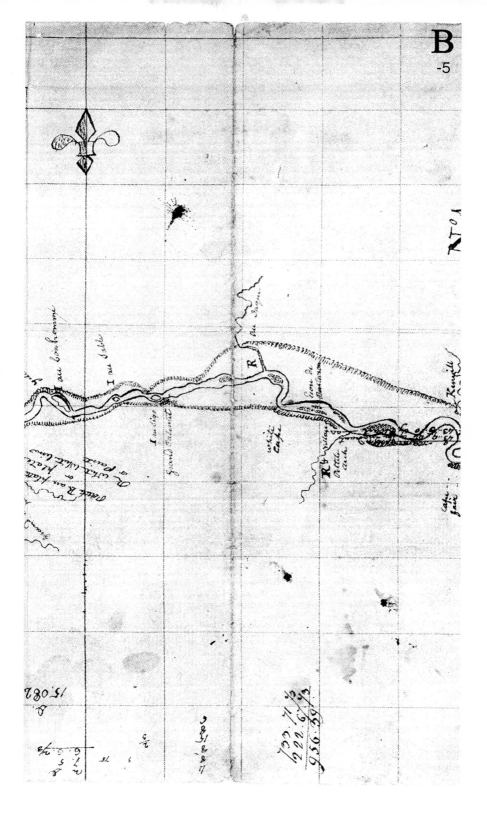

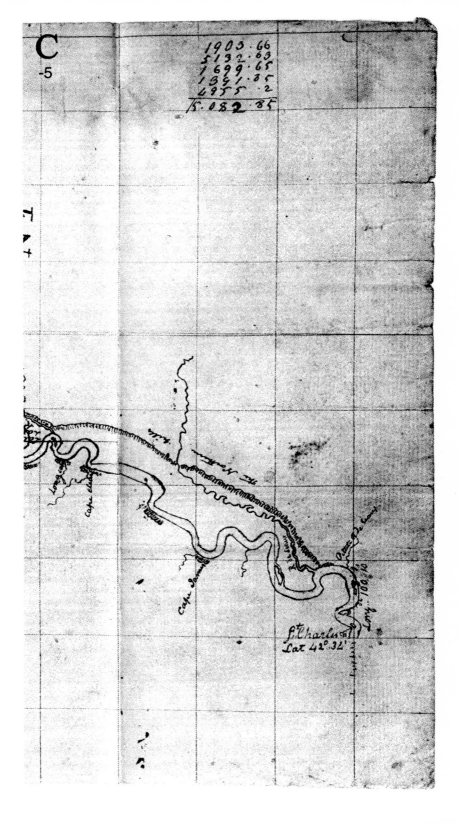

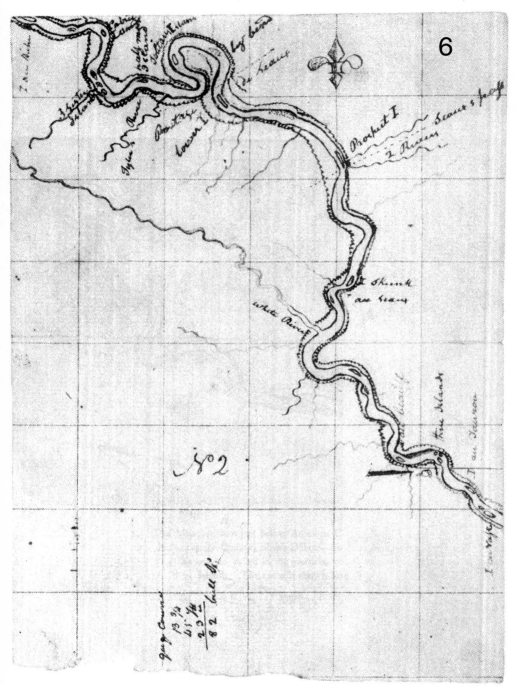

6. The Missouri River, in South Dakota, from Mud Island to Elk Island.
Route from September 10-23, 1804.
Mud Island (Isle au Vase) is Identified by Coues as Snag Island, not far above
Wheeler.   Elk Island (Isle au Biche), just below Medicine Knoll
River, is not charted on ordinary maps.
This chart is remarkably accurate and embraces the Big Bend of the Missouri.
Clark gives here the French forms of the names, evidently
those learned from his engages.

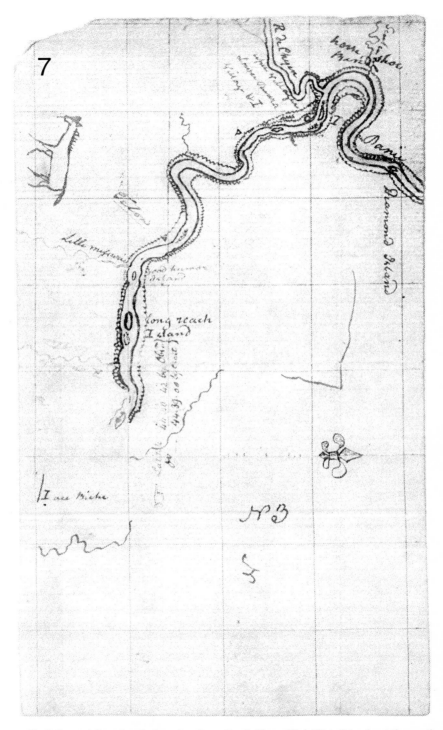

7. The Missouri from just below Antelope Creek [R on High Water] to about the northern
limit of Sully County, South Dakota—the Teton country.   Diamond Island is not
the one so called in the journals, but apparently the present H. Fishbeck
Island.   The route is shown for September 24-October 2, 1804.

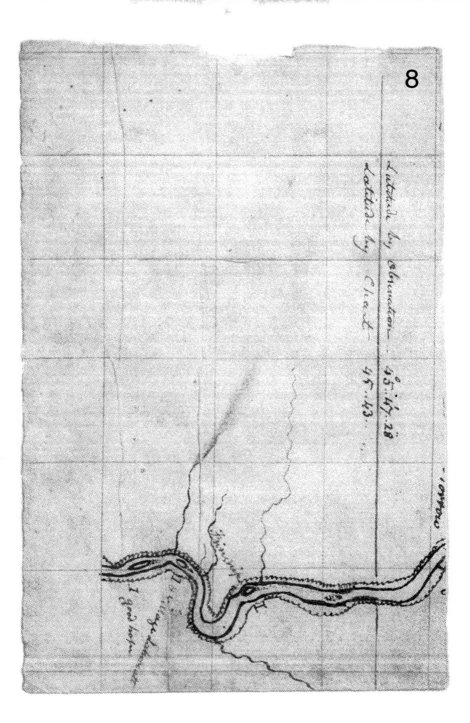

8. The Missouri, about forty miles above the mouth of Cheyenne River. The river coming in at the right, is Little Cheyenne. Lahoocatt Island is apparently the one now called Lafferty's ; the present Cheyenne Agency is just above this point. The route is shown for October 2-5, 1804.

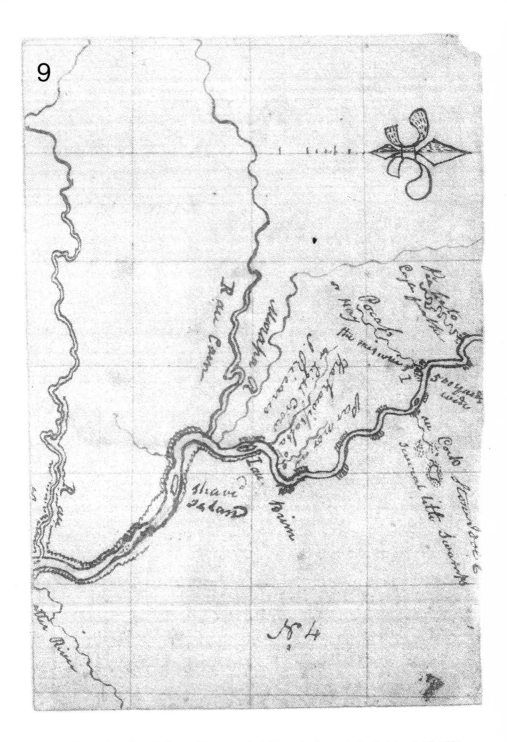

9. The region of the Arikara villages, on the Missouri—the route for October 7-15, 1804
The river at the bottom of the map is the present Moreau, in South Dakota, near the
boundary of North Dakota.   The lesser creeks bear the names of Arikara chiefs.

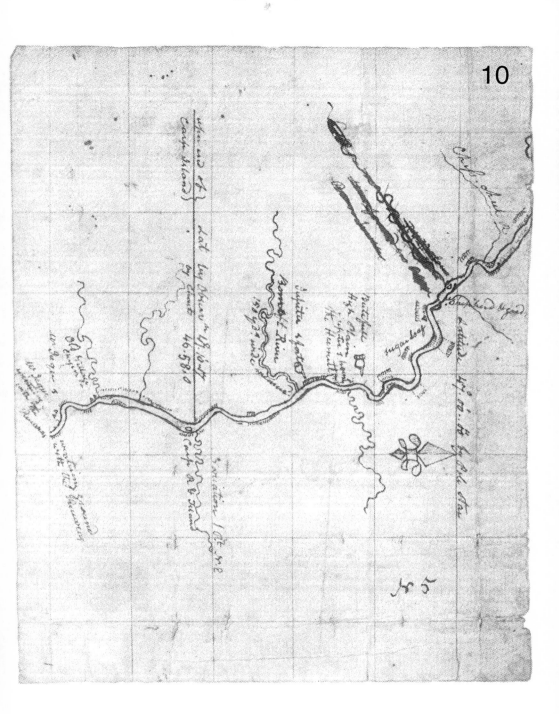

10. The Missouri in North Dakota, from about the point where it enters that state from South
Dakota to just below the site of Bismarck—the route for October 15-21, 1804. "Chess-
cheet" is the present Little Heart River ; the one about the centre of the map, is
intended for "Boulet," or Cannonball River.   Carp River is that now
known as Beaver Creek, in Emmons County, North Dakota.

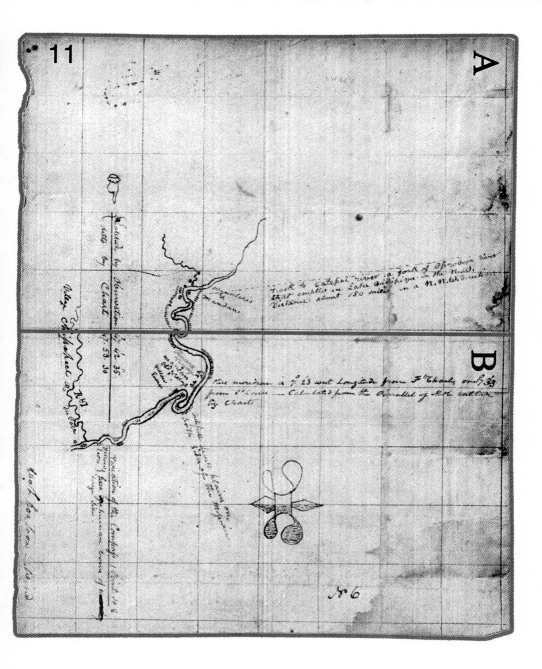

11. The Missouri, in the neighborhood of Fort Mandan ; showing the British
fur-trade trail towards the Assiniboin.

A
-11

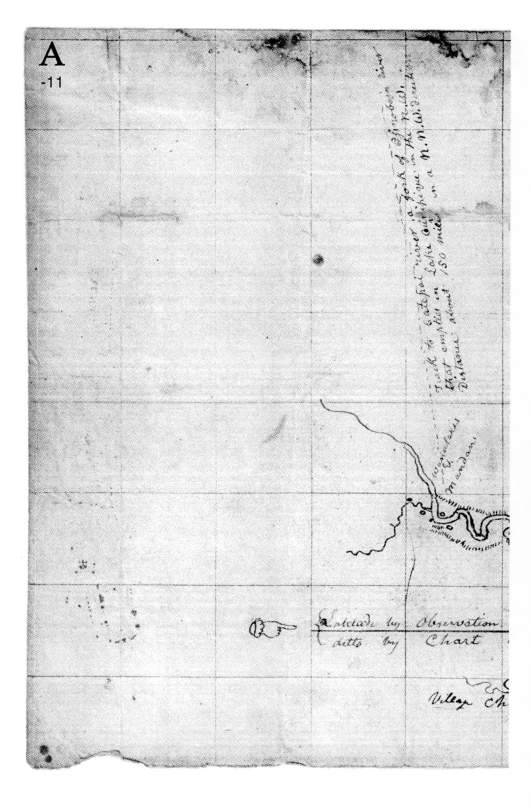

fork to Satesha river a fork of Missouri river
that emptied in Lake Outipique in a N.N.W. direction
Distance about 150 miles

Mandans
of the
Mountain

☞ Latitude by Observation
ditto by Chart

Village Ch

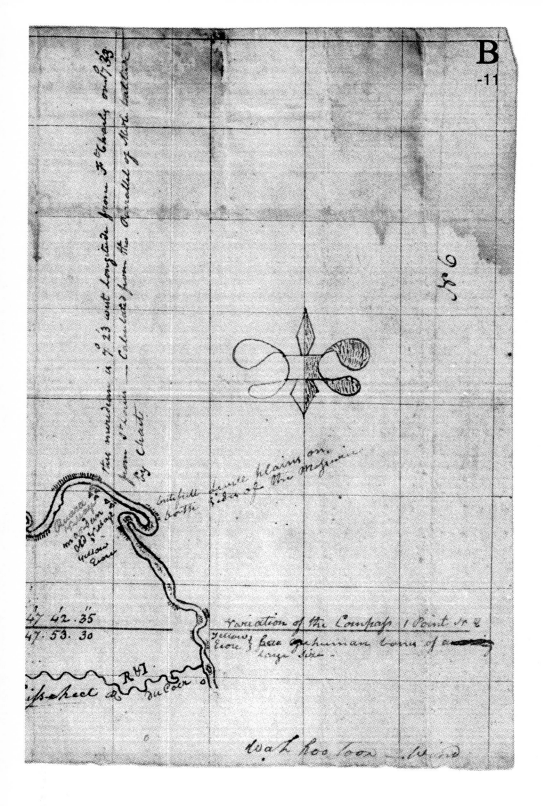

the meridian is 7° 23 west longitude from Fort Mandan on 7:35 from S. Louis — Calculated from the Parallel of Nore Latitude by Chart

N° 6

beautiful little plains on both sides of the engine

variation of the Compass 1 Point N°

Yellow Eore } face of human bones of a large size —

47 42. 35"
47. 53. 30

R47

fishood a   du Coeur o

Wah hoo toon — Wind

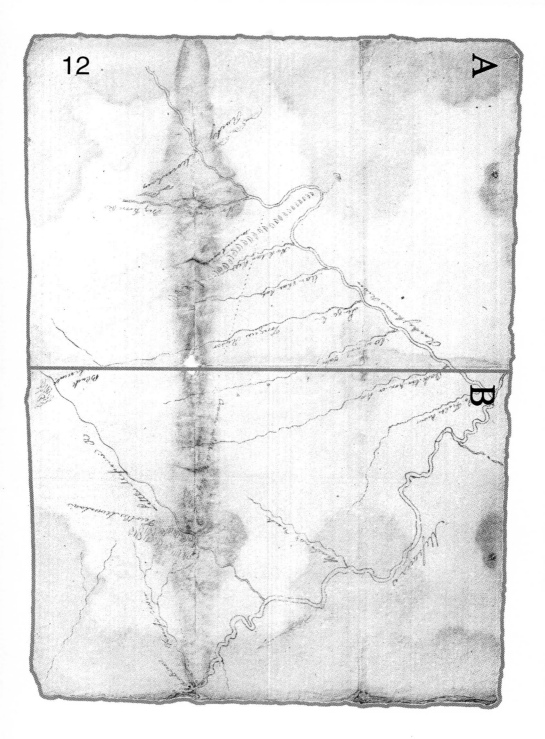

12. Trail from the Mandans to the Yellowstone—derived apparently from Indian information obtained at Fort Mandan.

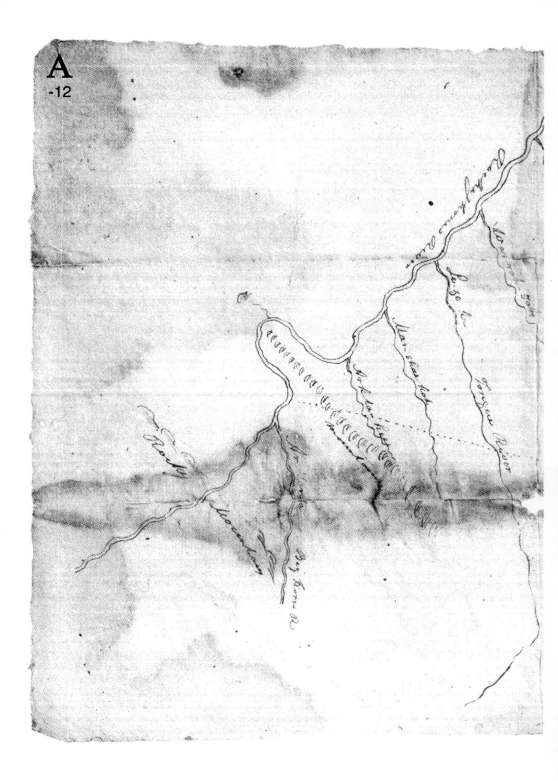

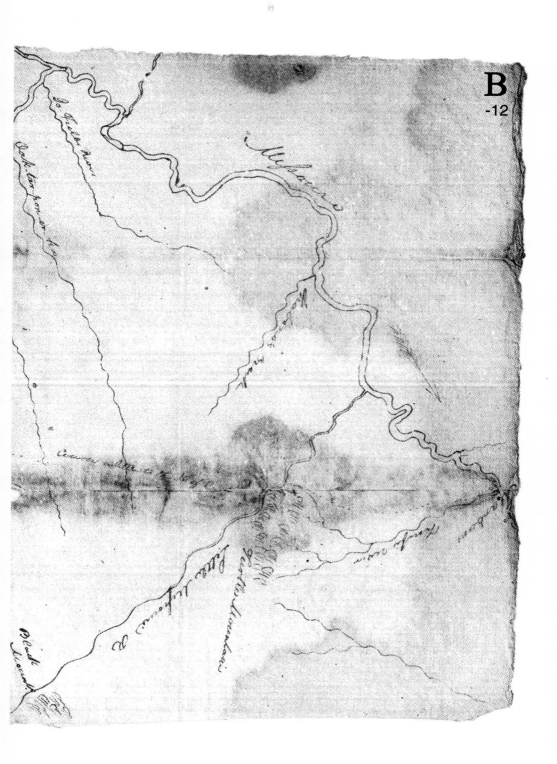

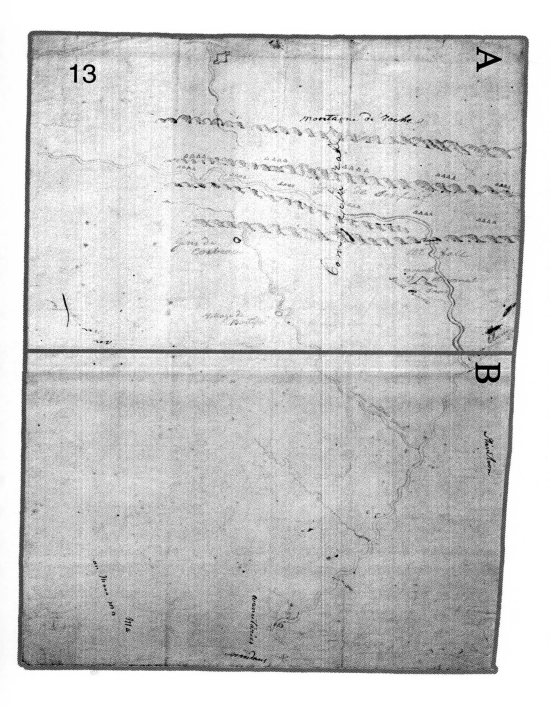

13. From the Mandans to the Rockies—Based apparently on information obtained from French and Indians at Fort Mandan.

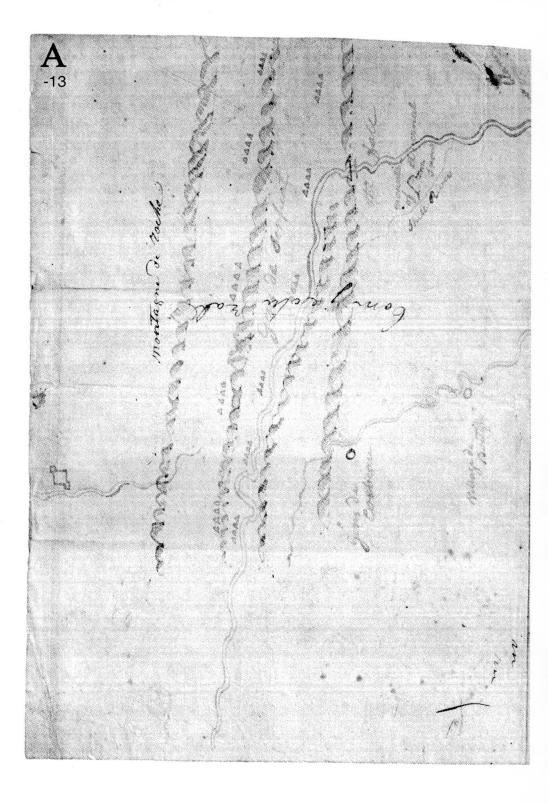

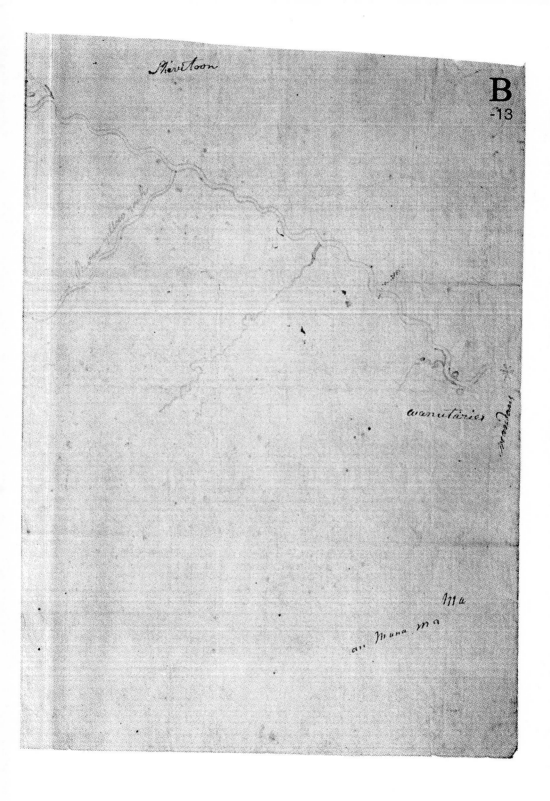

Shevitoon

B
-13

wanutaries

ma

an muna ma

14 Part I

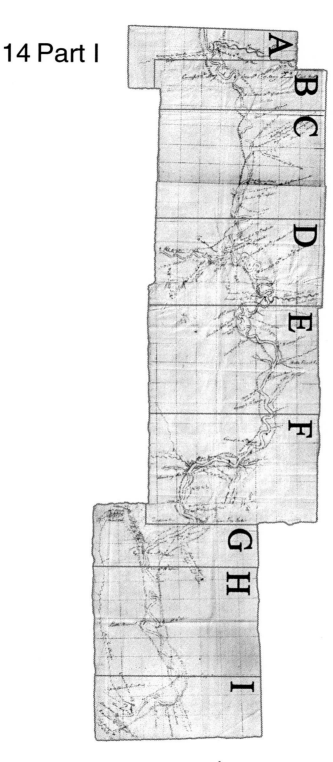

14. Sketch of the Missouri from Fort Mandan to the Rocky Mountains.—"From the 7th April to the 15th July, 1805."
Part I.

A
-14
Part I

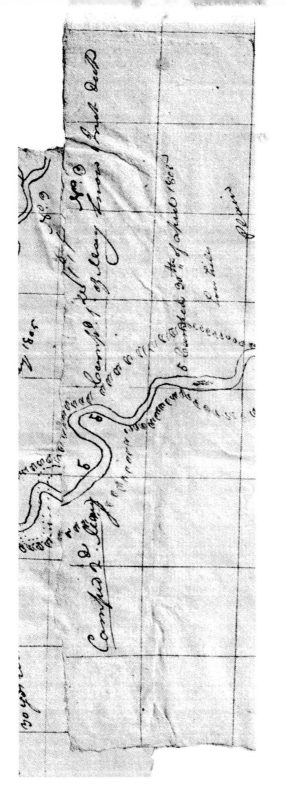

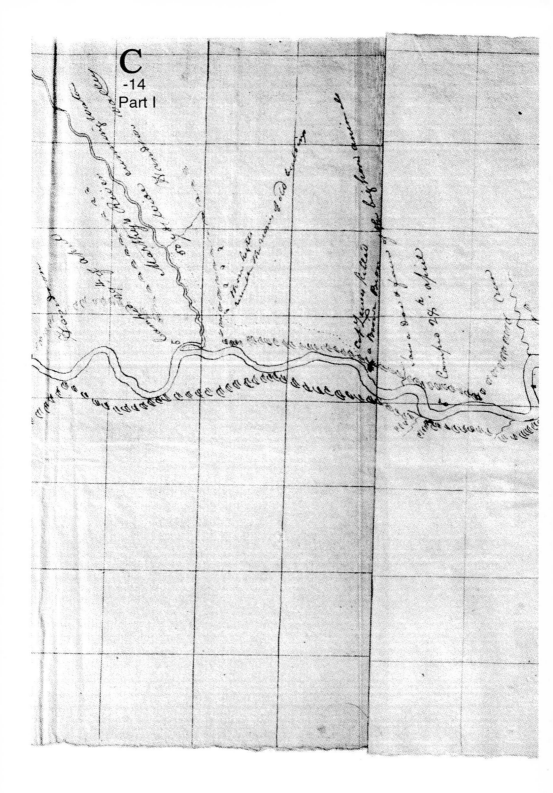

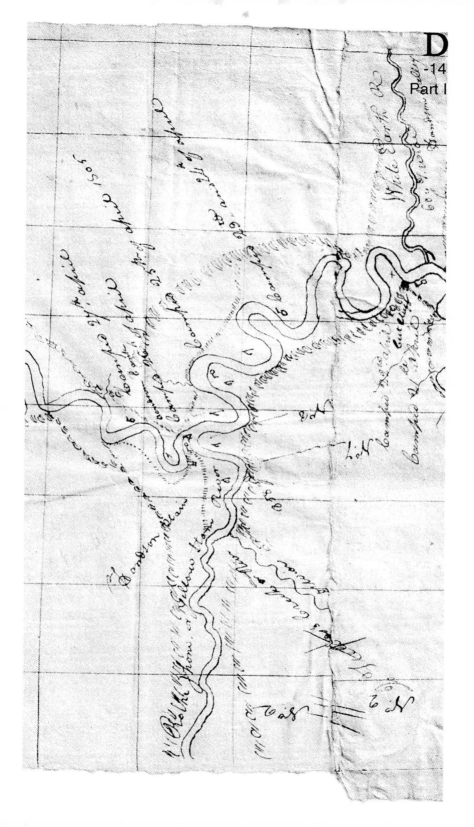

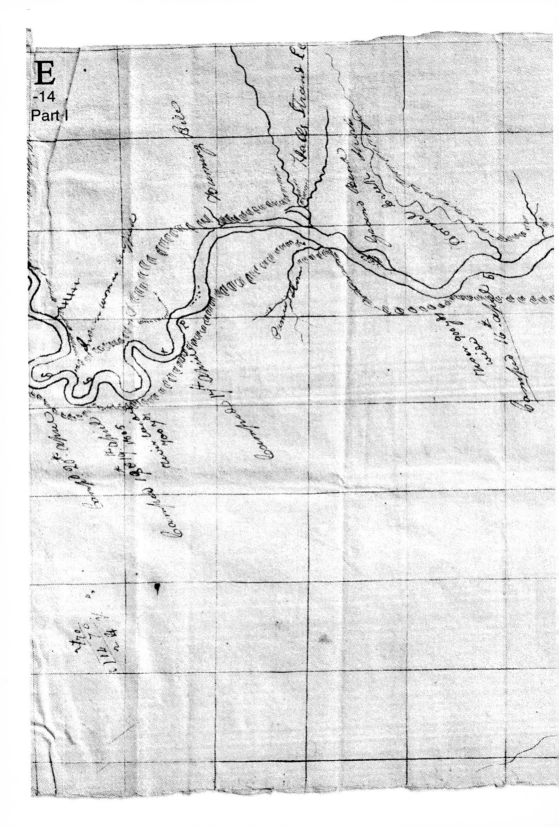

E
-14
Part I

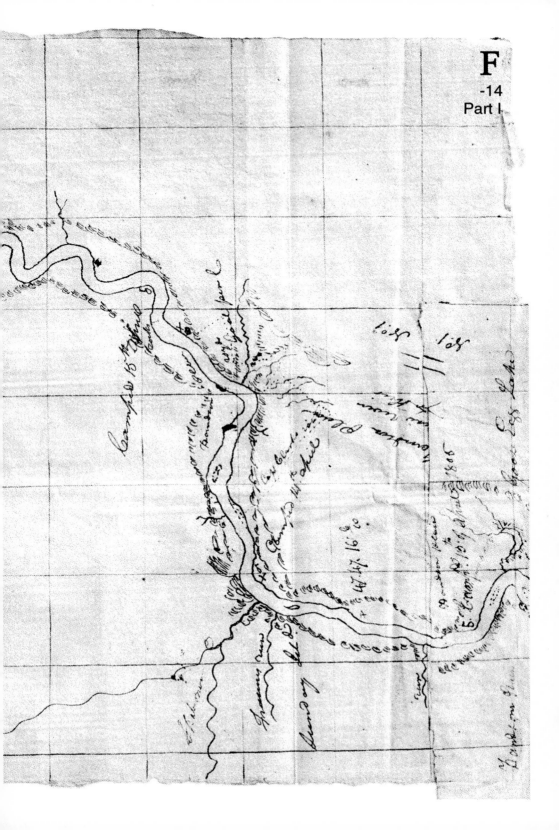

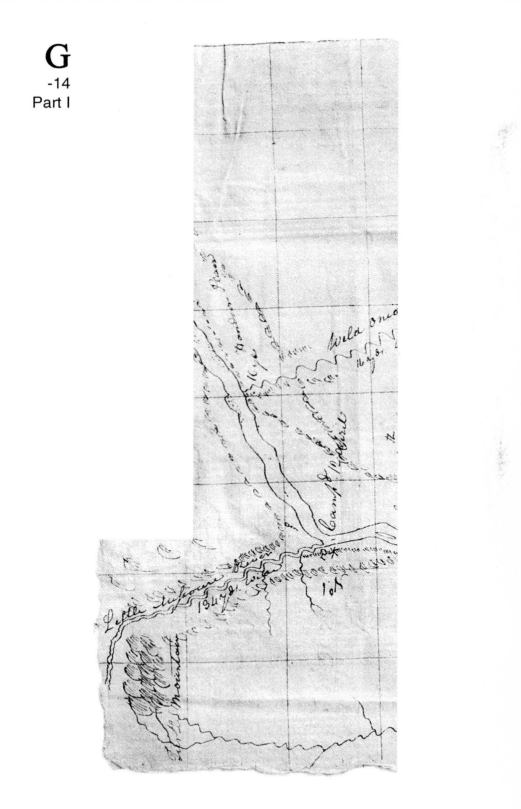

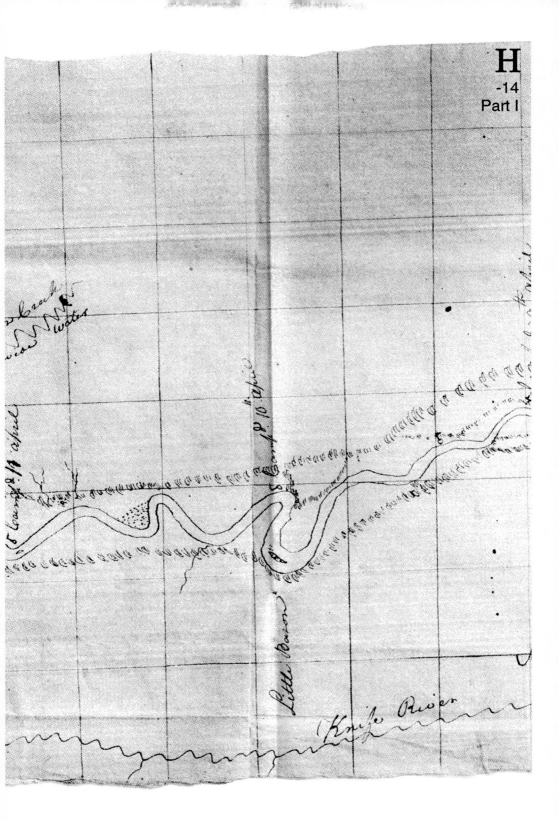

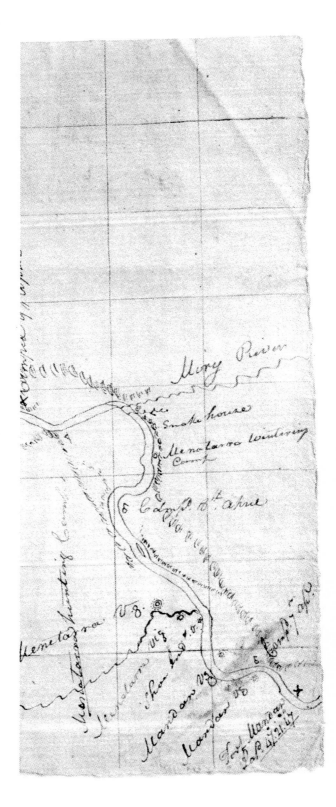

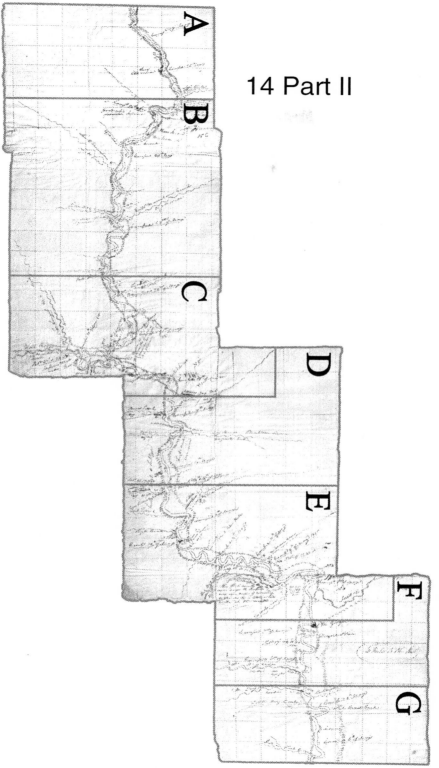

A

B

C

D

E

F

G

14 Part II

14.   Sketch of the Missouri from Fort Mandan to the Rocky Mountains.—" From the
7th 'April to the 15th July, 1805."
Part II.

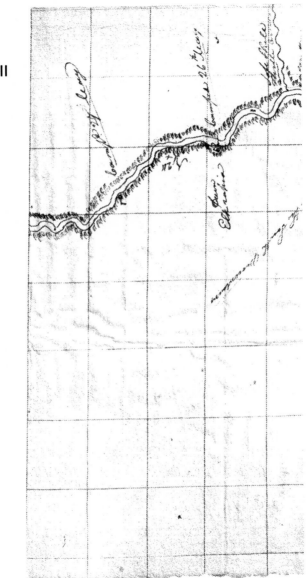

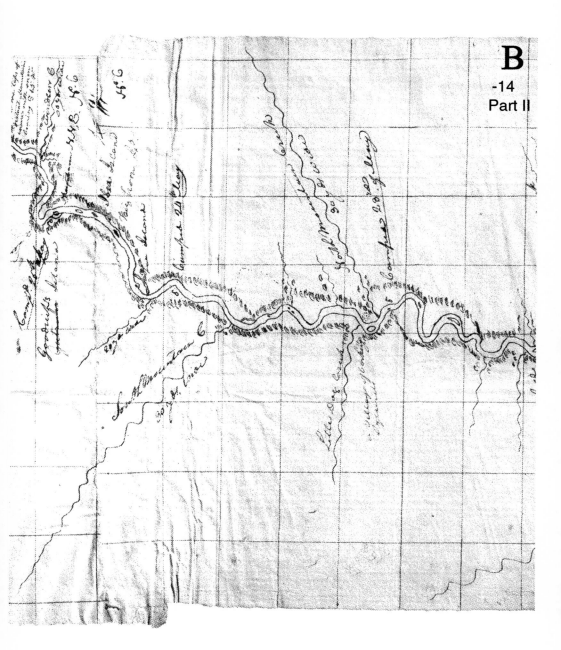

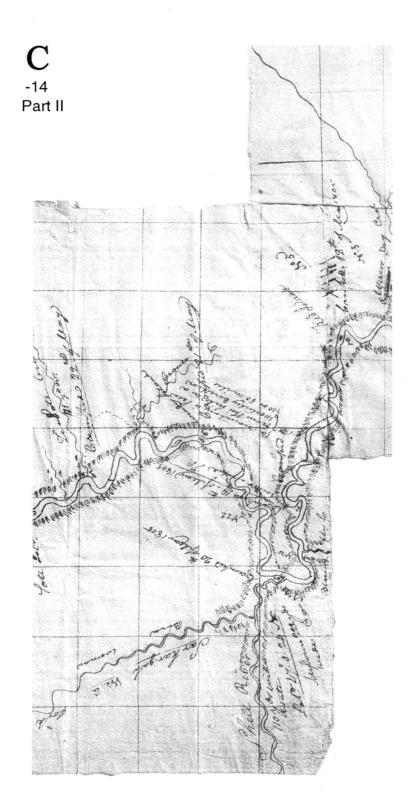

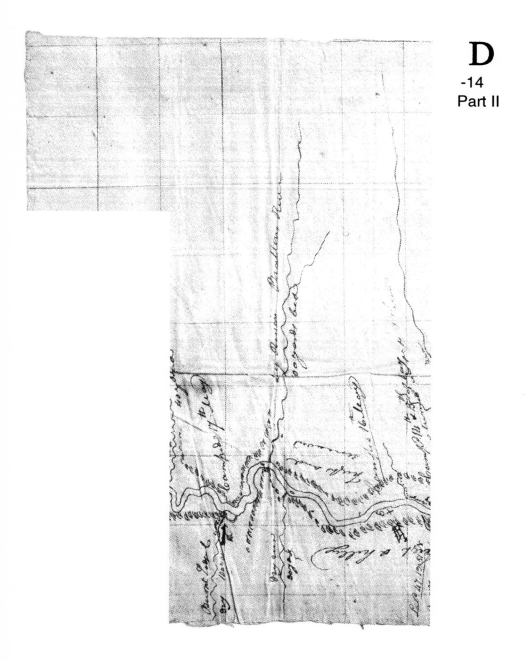

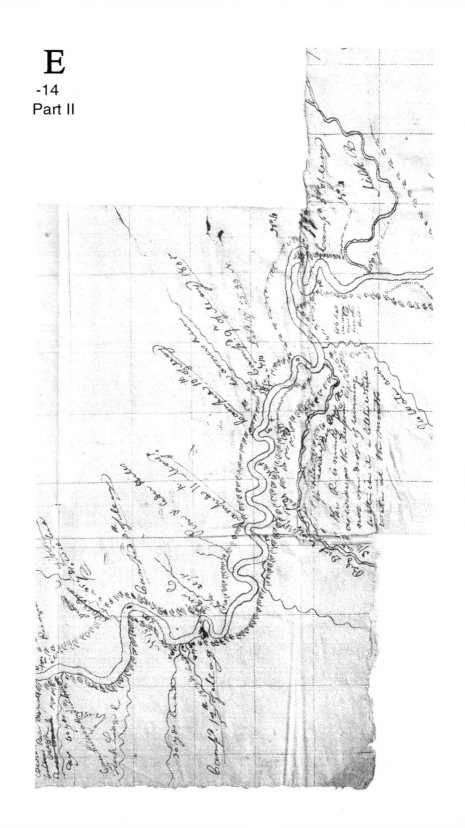

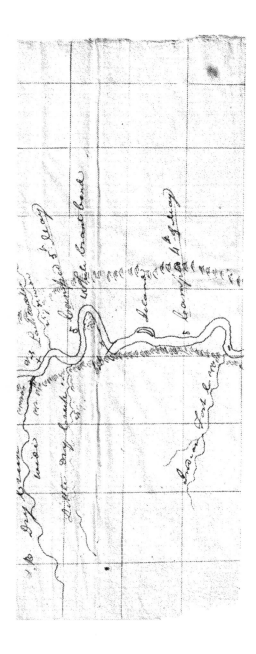

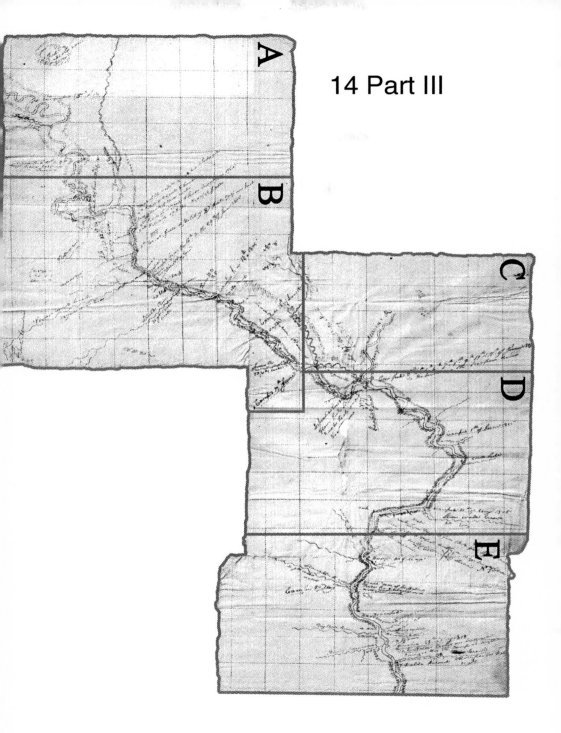

14 Part III

14.   Sketch of the Missouri from Fort Mandan to the Rocky Mountains.—" From the
7th April to the 15th July, 1805. "
Part III.

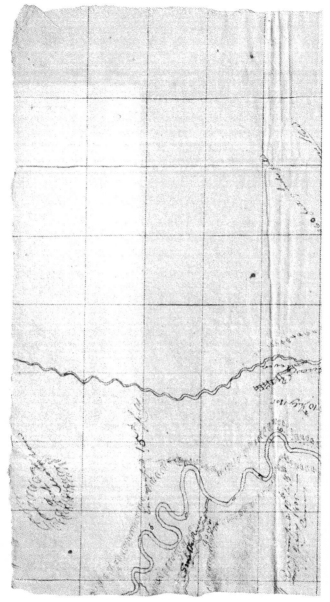

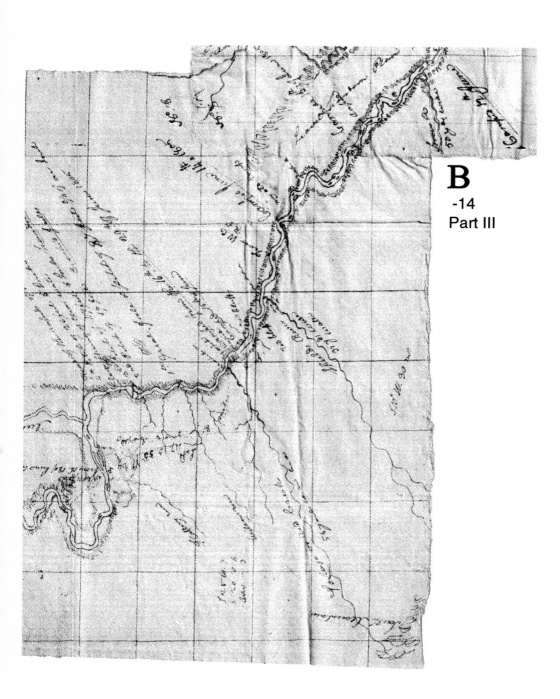

B
-14
Part III

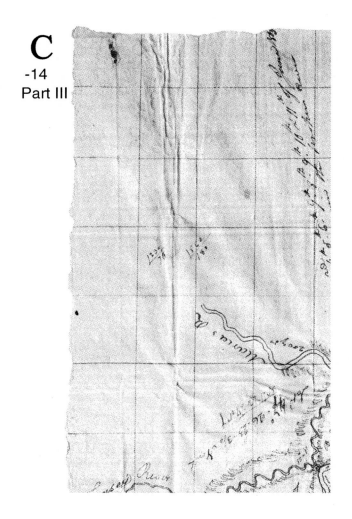

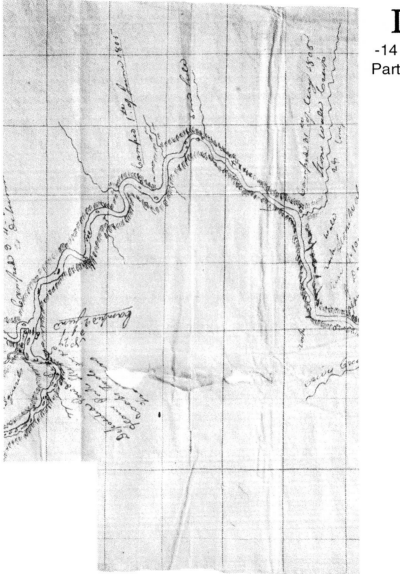

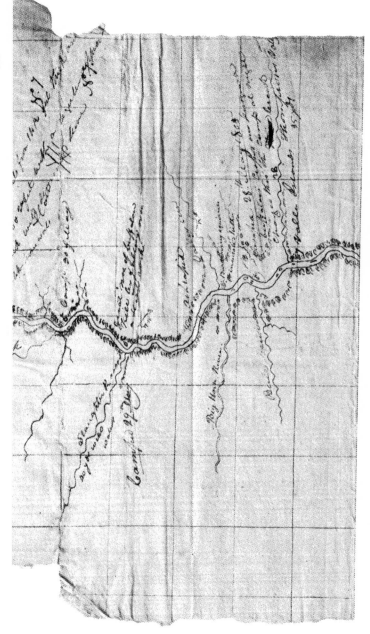

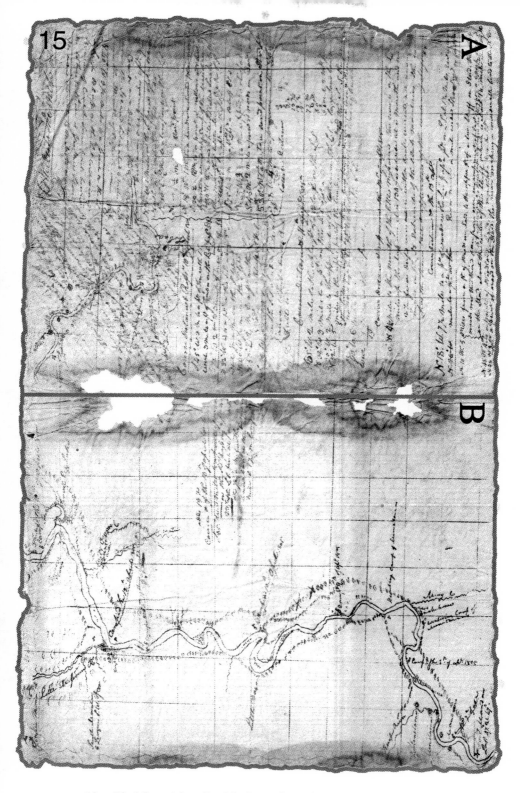

15. The Missouri from Fort Mandan to above Goose Egg Lake---the route
of April 7-13, 1805.

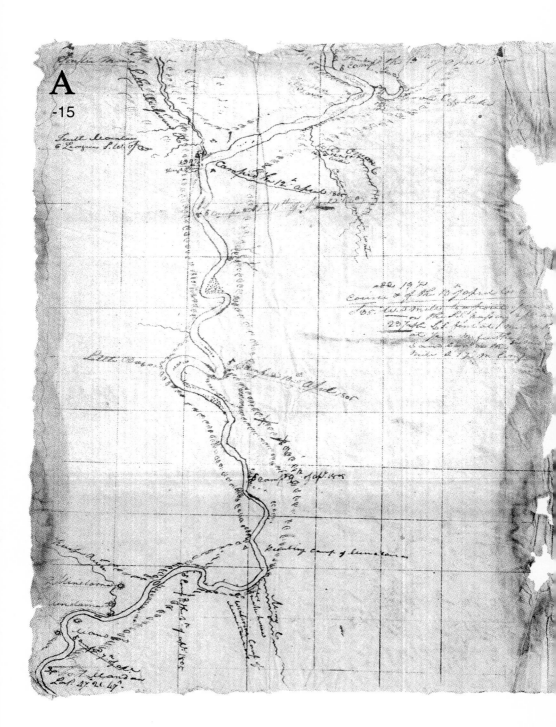

A

-15

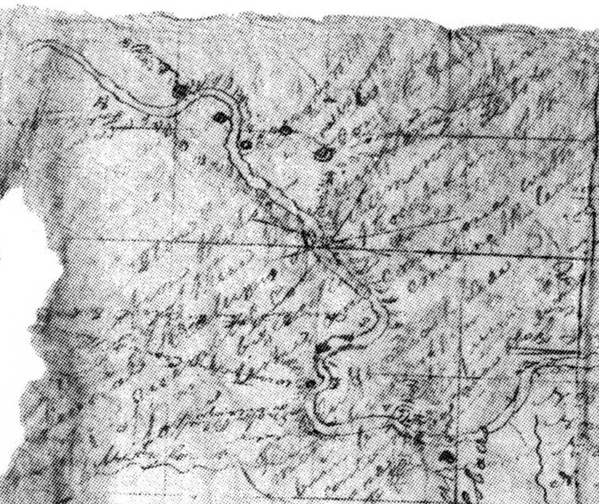

16. The Missouri from Goose Creek to White Earth River—the route of April 14-22, 1805.

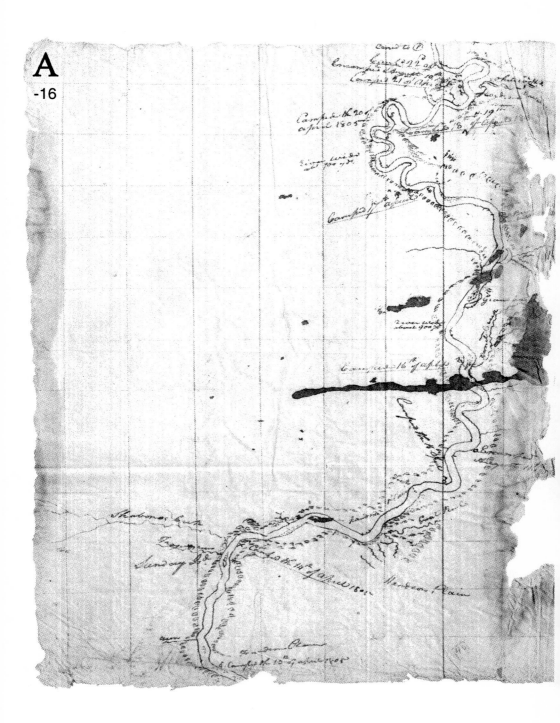

A

-16

Course Distance &c April 15 1805
S15° W. 2½ M. to the mouth of a small creek at
the upper point of a wood bottom on
Lard side

W. 3½ to a point opposite   on the Lard side
N. 85. W. ½ to a point Stard side opposite a bluff
N. 80. W. 1 to a point Stard passing a
bluff on Lard

W. 1 M. to a small Island corner point of
the river passing the borde of the hill
on both sides of this channel which
we call   Island from the
circumstance of our meeting at
our small part of the meal

N. 70. W. 3 to a point of woodland on Stard
this channel and its sand bar as
passing 1 of this distance
passed a run to Lards creek
on the Lard side

Course Distance &c April 15th 1805

South 2 miles to a pt of wood on the St
opposite a high hill on Stard

N. 18 W. 5 M. to a pt of wood on St
                 opposite a high hill on Lard

N. 80. E. 2 from the upper point of a bluff
on the S. S. beyond the upper pt
the wood and the

point of woodland at Stard

N. to a point of wood on Stard 52

N. 30. E. 2½ M. to a point of woodland on S S
N. 10. W. ½ along the Lard point
N. 18. W. ½ to
N. 12. W. 1½ miles to the point of a bluff on St S
½ mile below which a large creek falls in 33
N. 62. W. 2 miles to a high bluff point St S
N. 75 W. 3 miles to a point of woodland 33
W. ½ to a Sand beach on the St

Courses distances &c April 16th 1805
S. W. 3 M. to a point of woodland Stard S S
opposite to a bluff Lard S S
S. 60. W. 2½ M. to a point of woodland Lard S S
S. 60. W. 3½ M. to a point of W. on St Stard
opposite to a bluff Lard commencing
1 mile below it
N. 25. W. 2½ miles to a point of woodland Lard S S
S. 70. W. 4½ miles to a S. point on St
S. 70 W. 1½ along wood bar on the Lard
to a point of woodland on St

S. 65. W. along the Lard point of woodland
Miles 18

April 17th 1805

S. 70. W. M. 3 Miles to a willow
on Stard side
S. 75. W. ½ M. to a point on St side of
N. 75. W. 3 Mile to a wood in a bend
N. 50. W. 3½ Miles to a point of woodland on
S. 65. W. 3½ of a mile to a point of woodland S S
to a bluff on Lard side
above which a creek falls in
Lard about 10 yards wide
N. 82. W. 3¼ to a willow point on Lard
S. 85. W. 3½ M. to a point of
opposite a bluff on St S
passing a creek on Lard
W. 1 M. along the Lard point of woodland
a high bluff on Stard side
which a small creek
S. 40. M. along the same point of woodland
S. 30. W. ½ Mile along the Lard point to a
S. 14. W. 4 miles to the upper point of
timber on Stard side
S. 28. W. 2 miles to a point on Lard side
we encamped for the
26 Miles

Course Distance &c April
South 3 M. to a Sand point on the
N. 75° W. 2½ to a wood point on
Stard
N. 85. W. ½ M. along the Stard
N. 8. 2 M. to a Sand point St S
S. 60. W. 1 Mile to a point of willow
S. 65. W. ½ mile along the St point
point of timber turn a
route to a bluff on Lard
N. 25. W. 2 miles to a point of woodland
the Lard an Stard
S. 50. W. 1½ miles to a point meadow
where we encamped for the night
12
Course Distance &c the W

North 10 miles a bluff on Stard of a
a low point of a low wood bottom
W. 4 M. to a timbered point on
N. 85 ½ M. along
S. 45. 2 M. to a point

17. The Missouri from   White Earth River to twenty miles above Marth's River, showing the mouth of the Yellowstone—the route of April 22-30, 1805.

Courses and distances 21st April

miles

S. E. 1½ to a sand point Stard. side.
opposite to a bluff Lard —

S. 5° W. ½ to a point of high timber on S.S.
opposite to a bluff —

N. 60° W. 3½ to a willow point on Lard. side
opposite to a bluff on Stard.

N. 60° W. ... to a point of timber on Std. side ...
just below which on the Lard. side
a creek falls in the ... discharge
... no water at present

N. 25° E. 2 miles to a point of willow land
opposite to a high bluff on Std. S.

N. 16° W. 2 to the upper part of a bluff on S.S.
in a ... to S.P.

S. 90° W. 3 miles to the upper part of the
Stard. bottom at a bluff on S.S.

... 16 S. Pass? a pt. on the L.S.

Course & distance 22d aprl

N. 60° W. 2 to a pt. of wood land on the S.S.
along the S. point of wood

S. ... 1 mile to the lower part of a bluff
on the S side in a bend

S. 20° W. 2 miles to the upper part
of the bluff on the S side

N. 60° W. 1 mile to a wood in the bend on N.S.

N. 30° E. 2 m. to the pt. of willow on the N.S.

N. 65° E. 1½ m. to an object in the bend on
miles 11 the L.S. Saw many beaver

Course & distance 23 aprl

N. 25° S. 2 7 m. to a pt. of timbered land
on the N. side

South 1½ m. on the S.S. of a wood in
a bend Black Aproach

S. 78° W. 4 m. to the upper part of a coppice of
wood in a bend to the S.S

S. 44° E. 4 m. to a point of high timber in
a Land bend

S. 25° W. 1½ to a point of timbered land
10½ on Lard side in a bend ...
miles to a point of ... land S.
... two miles from commencement of the
course ... on Stard side

Course & distance the 25th of April

N. 63° W. 2 ½ m. to a point on the
L. side of wood land

West 1¾ to a view in a bend to S.S.
South 1½ m. to a low bluff S. S in a bend

East 2½ miles to a pt. of timber on L.
side ... have S8

S. 28° E. 2¾ m. on the S of willow or gravel

S. 20° W. 1 m. on the S of a low bluff S side L.

N. 65° W. 3 m. to the upper part of the timber
in a bend to the L side

N. 72° W. 2 ½ m. to the lower ... of
timber in a bend to ...
14

Course and distance 26th aprl

N. 45° E. 2½ m. to a pt. of wood land
on the Starboard side

S. 60° W. 1 ½ m. on the S. S. of a bluff

N. 75° W. 3 miles to a ... on the
S side ...

South 1 mile to the junction of the
Rochejone & Missourie Rivers
3

Course Distance of 27 of April

S. 9° E. ... ...
... on the L.S. ...
West 1 mile to the lower part of a timber in a bend to the L side

N. 32° W. 3 miles along a wood to the
... on the L side
... a bank side S.

West 3 miles to a point on the S S
8 Camped at 1 mile on Stard

Course & distance of 28th april

North 2½ miles to timbered point on Stard.

N. 40° W. 1 m. on the L point of wood the
opposite a high bluff S. S

S. 56° W. 2¾ miles to a bluff point on the
L. ... opposite a point of wood S.

S. 45° W. 1 mile to the center of a bend on Lard

N. 25° W. 3 mile to a point of timber land S.
passing a point on Std at 1½ mile
S. 18° W. 2 miles to the lower point of the timber in
a bend on Stard side —

S. 4° W. 4 miles to a point of woodland on Std.

S. 10° W. 2 to a high bluff point on Lard the
river making a considerable bend to S.S.

N. 80° ... 2¼ miles to a point of woodland Lard

N. 45° W. 1 mile to a high bluff point on Stard

S. 60° W. 3 m. to a point of woods, on Std side
2½

Course Distance 29 April 1805

N 45 W 3½ to a point of woodland on the
opposite a high Bluff timber passing
with 2½ a pt of woodland on the Stard

S 80 W 1½ on the Stard a high Shark of
Cliff opposite a point of wood
Capt Lewis killed a yellow bear

S 45 W 2 to a point of wood land on the Lard

S 55 W 3 a high bluff opposite on the Stard
to a point of timber Lard side high
bluff on Star

N 60 W 1½ to a bluff point on Stard in a Stard bend

S 30 W 3 Miles to the upper part of the high timber
on Lard side in a Lard bend of the river

S 85 W 1½ to a point of timbered land on Stard
opposite to a bluff

N 55 W 3½ to the commencement of a bluff on Stard
passing a Sand point on Lard at 2 2 miles

S 75 W 1½ to a point of woodland on Lard passing
passing the point of a sandbar on Stard
the river making a deep bend to the South

N 75 W 3 Miles to the entrance of a river on
Stard in a Stard bend encamped for the
night

25 Miles

Courses and distances of April 30th 1805

S 15 W 2½ miles to a point of timber Stard passing
Lard a point at 3/4 of a mile

S 22 W 1½ to the upper point of the high timber on
Stard side in a bend Lth the commencement
of the bluff on Stard

S 85 W 1 to a point of timbered Land on Stard
opposite to a bluff on Lard

S 75 W 1½ to the lower point of the timber at the
upper part of the bluff on Lard side
in a Lard bend

N 40 W 5 to a sand point of a sand bar on Lard
passing a willow point at 2 M and
a large sandbar on Stard side

S 45 W 3½ to a point of woodland on Stard passing
opposite to a bluff on Lard the river
making a considerable bend to Lard

N 70 W 3 to a point of woodland Lard passing
at the commencement of the same
a large sand bar on Stard in a Lard bend

S 2 W 1½ to the upper part of the high timber
on the Stard side
with 1½ a pt of high timber on the Lard side a sand Island S S

24

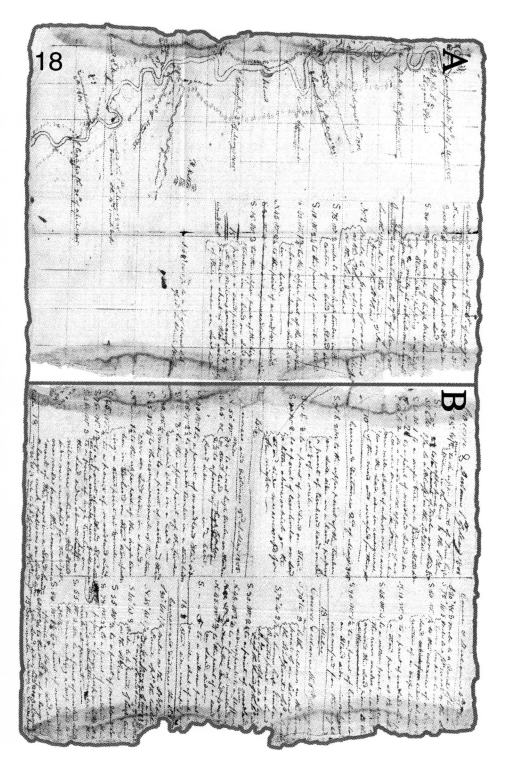

18. The Missouri from Martha's River to just below Milk River---the route of
April 30—May 7, 1805.

A
-18

Encamped the 7th of May 1805

Course and distances of the 6th of May &c

Elegant Plains

S. 80. W. to a clump of high trees in a ... Stard. side, passing a ... at 2 miles at which we encamp... for the night

Encamped the 6th of May 1805

Course and distances the 7th of May 1805

N. 2 miles to a point of woods ...

S. 75. W. 2 miles to some high timber in the center of a bend on Stard side

S. 10. W. 2¼ to the point of a sandbar Stard.

S. 40. W. 1¾ to the upper part of the high timber in ... Lard side in a bend

N. 45. W. 2½ to the point of a sandbar Lard.

Encamped August 5th 1805

S. 15. W. 3 to the upper part of the high timber in a bend on Lard. side passing a sand point on Stard at 2 Miles encamped ... 2 miles short of the end of this course on Lard side

Wind hard

Island

Encamped 9th of May 1805

H. Hill

Encamped the 1st of May 1805

Encampd 2d May

Encamped the 30th of April 1805

Course & Distance 1st of May 1805

N. 88° W. ¾ to the upper point of som high
timber in the bend to the Stb'd

S. — 8° — 2¾ to the upper point of timber on Lar'd S.
S. 26 W. 1½ to a Bluff on the Lar'd side
S. 60 W. 1 to a single tree on a point Stb'd side
N. — — 2¾ to a point of woodland Lar'd side
N. 60° W. 2, to a wood at the upper point of an
Island Some mile short of which we came
for on the Lar'd side in consequence
10 of this wind we encamped for the night

Courses & Distances 2d of May 1805

S. 70° E. 2 M. to the upper point of the timber
on Lar'd side in a bend, passing
a point of timbered land on Stb'd
at ½ of a mile —
S. 10 E. ½ to a point of woodland on Star'd
S. 20 W. 2 to a point of low timber on Lar'd
a little above which on the
Stb'd side we encamped for
the night
4½

Courses and distances 3rd of May 1805

N. 50 W. ¾ to a point high timber on Star'd
S. 65 W. 2½ to a point of high timber on
Lar'd side — in a bend.
N. 40 W. 1 to a point of woodland Stb'd side
N. 55 W. 2½ to some low timber in a Star'd bend
S. — — 3 to the upper point of the timber
on Lar'd side in a bend —
N. 80 W. ½ mile to a point of woodland Star'd
S. 45 W. 1¼ to the commencement of the timber on Lar'd side in a bend
N. — — 1½ to the upper part of the high timber in the bend on Star'd side; passing a Star'd point at 1 mile —
S. 65 W. ½ to a point of woodland Lar'd
S. 75 W. 1½ to a point of woodland Star'd
S. 45 W. 3 to a point of high timber on the Lar'd side about half a mile above which on the Star'd side we encamped for the night, one mile from the commencement of this course in a Lar'd bend a large creek falls in on Lar'd side
miles 18   S. 60 W. ½ mile to a point of wood on the Star'd

Course & Distance 4th of May 1805

S. 80° W. 3 mile to a Point of timber
S. 72° W. 5 mile to a pit wood on the Star'd
S. 50 W. 1½ to the entrance of a Creek Star'd side about the center of a deep bend
N. 10 W. 3 to a point of woodland Star'd a Star'd point at 1½ mile
S. 45 W. 4 to a willow point on Star'd this river makes a considerable around the Lar'd point to the
S. 70 W. 1½ to a point of timbered land on Star'd side encamped for the night
18 Miles

Course & distance the 5th of May 1805

S. 70 W. 3 both willows on the Lar'd point of an Island and the Star'd point of sd.
S. 72 W. 2 to some high timber Star'd point in a bend opposite a Star'd the head of the Island
S. 30 W. 2¼ to a point of woodland Lar'd side opposite to a low
S. 48 W. 2½ to a point of woodland along the Lar'd point
N. 45 W. ½ to the point of a Sand on Lar'd side
S. — — 5 to a willow point one mile short of which Star'd side encamped
16

Courses and distances the 6th

S. 30 W. 1½ miles on the Star'd side point of sd. the timber
N. 45 W. 1½ to a Sand point
S. 60 W. 3 mile to a point of high timber on the Star'd
S. 55 W. 3 to a point of woodland Star'd
S. 78 W. 2½ to a point of woodland Star'd passing a large creek on Lar'd side at a mile but little water in this creek at present.
S. 55 W. 2 M. to a point of woodland Lar'd the river making a deep bend to the
S. 50 W. 1½ to a point of woodland Star'd opposite a bluff on Lar'd side
S. 60 W. ½ to the mouth of a large creek on Lar'd side, but 200 yds wide no water running

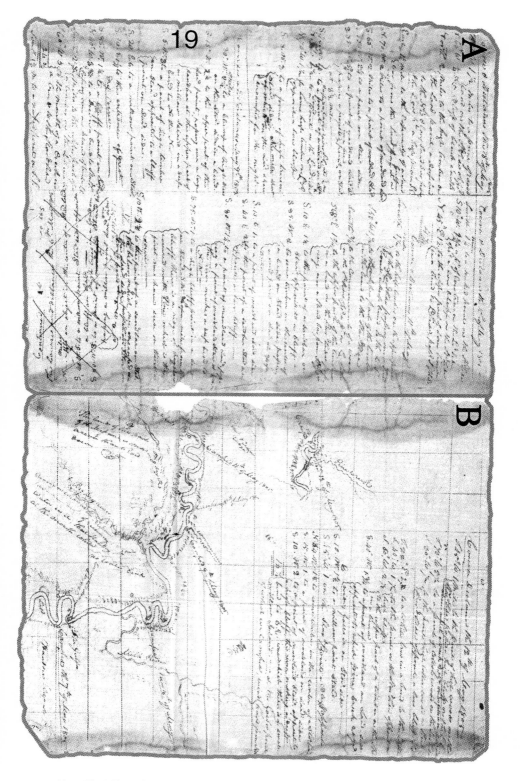

19.   The Missouri from below Milk River to Pine Creek—the route of May 8-12, 1805.

Course & Distance the 18th of May 1805

S 88° W. 1½ Miles to a point of wood land on the Stard side of the river
S. 65° W. ¼ 58 to Bluff of black earth Stard
North 2 Miles to the high timber on the Lard point, a deep bend to the N.E. & Lary Sand bar from the Lard to a high plain S.
East ½ mile to the Extremity of a sand bar from the Lard point at
N. 70° W. a miles to a point of woodland Lard
S. 65° W. 2 Mile to a point of woodland Stard
S. 35° W. 2½ to a point on Stard side
S. 85° W. ½ to a point of woodland Lard B passing a project point on Stard at 3½ mile
S. 44° W. ¼ to a point of woodland on Stard
N. 45° W. 1½ to a point on the Lard side
N. 70° W. 1½ to some high timber on the Stard opposit a low bluff
S. 18° W. 3 to a point of high trees on Stard side, a mile short of which on the Lard shore Encamped for the night

Courses and Distances May 9th 1805
S. 30° W. 2¼ to a clump of high trees on the Stard side in a bend
S. 15° W. 2½ to the upper point of the Stard point, passing a large sand bar at the upper part of a willow Island in a deep bend to the N.
S. 5° W. 3 to a point of high timber on Stard opposit to a bluff point on Lard side.
S. 20° E. 6 to a willow point on Stard
S. 10° E. 1½ to the entrance of great dry river
S. 85° W. 1½ to a bluff point on Lard
N. 40° W. 3½ to a view in a bend to Stard passing over an Island of timber
South 2 Miles to the upper part of a timber on the Lard side
S. 60° W. 3 to the mouth of a creek in a bend to the Stard side
                          24 ¾
South 1½ Miles to a naked point on S.S.

Course & Distance the 18th of May 1805
South 1½ to a naked point on the Stard side
S 10° W. 4½ a Stard of Cotton trees on the Lard side opposit a low bluff on the Stard side
N. 45° E. 1½ to the upper part of some timber in a bend to Stard side, passd S. of

Course & Distances 11th of May
South 1½ to the high timber on the upper part of the Stard side passing over a sand bar a deep bend to the Lard
S. 45° W. 1½ to the upper part of the timber on the bend to the Stard side
South ¾ to the commencement of a wood on the Stard side, passing a point on Lard
S. 68° E. 1¾ to the upper part of the timber in a bend on the Stard side, passing over a sand bar from Stard
S. 10° E. 1½ to the point of a sand bar on Stard opposite to a bluff
S. 85° W. 2 to some timber in the center of a bend on Stard side, passing a sand point on Lard at 3½ M
S. 10° E. 1 to a point of woodland Lard side
S. 40° E. 2½ to the point of a sand bar Stard side opposite a low bluff
S. 80° W. 1½ to a point of woodland Lard, passing a point of woodland Stard at the river makes a deep bend to N.W.
S. 75° W. 1 to a high bluff point in a bend on Stard S.W. one mile from the bluff there is a ridge or highland covered with Pine which is the first we have seen on this river
S. 10° W. 2½ to the point of a sand bar on Stard, the below which we encamped on the Stard side
S. 45° W. 1½

Course Descending the 12th of May 1805

S. 45° W. 1 Mile to the Point of high woods on the Lar[board]
S. 70° W. 2½ to a pound of Cotton wood on the Star[board]
S. 30° W. 7½ to the point high Cotton wood on the Lar[board]
S[tar]. & Lar[board] Side opposit a low bluff

T. 22° E. 2½ to a White tree in a bend to the Lar[board]
S. 40° W. 1½ to the point on the Star Side opposit a
S. 60° W. 2½ high bluff
to the upper point of a timber on the Star
S. 40° W. 1¾ to a point of woodland on Lar[board] side
opposit to which Mine Creek 20 y[ar]ds
wide, falls in on Star side
S. 10° W. 1½ to a willow point Star[board]
S. 45° W. 1 on the Star point a D[itt]o Lar[board]
N. 54° W. 1½ to some timber in the center of a Star[board]
S. 15° W. 1 to a point of woodland on Lar[board] side
S. 10° W. 2 to a point of woodland Star[board], opposit to
a high bluff, the river making a deep
bend to S.E. in which there is a small
willow Island. at the lower point
of which we Camped, wind hard from w[est]

Camp[e]d the 7th of May 1805

Campd the 7th of May 1805

20

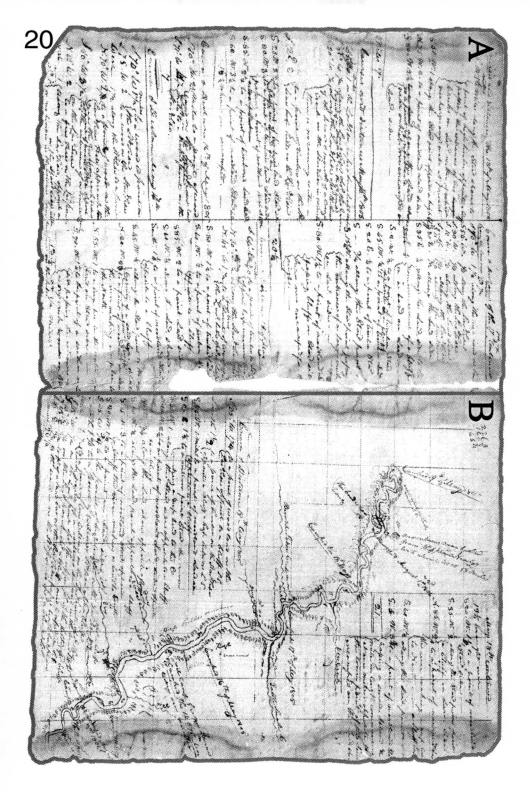

20. The Missouri from Pine Creek to just below Musselshell River—the route of May 13-19 1805, with indications of return camps in August, 1806.

Courses and distances the 18th of May 1805

S.55. W. 1/2 mile along the Stard shore to a
    point of high timber opposite a bluff
    passing the entrances of two _____
    creeks on Lard neither of which
    discharge any water at present
S.30. W. 1 along the Stard point opposite a high
N.25. W. 2. to a point of woodland Lard side.
S.80. W. 2 1/2 along the Stard shore
    to a point of woodland
    near which we encamped on
    Lard side.

9 Miles 7/8.

Courses and distances May 17th 1805

S.55. W. 1 on the Lard side, passed some bluff
    S.70. W. 1/2 along the Lard side opp. the lower
    point of an Island in the ground
S.20. W. 1/2 along the Lard side opp the head
    of the Island & mouth of a large
    creek on the Stard side in which
    there is no running water
S.12. E. 3 to a point of timber on the Stard
    some bluff hills on the Lard side
S.20. W. 2 1/2 to a point of timbered land Stard
S.80. W. 3 to a bluff on Lard side
    to a point of timbered land Lard side
    passing a point of woodland Stard
S.55. W. 2 1/2 to a point of timbered land Lard
S.60. W. 3 1/2 to a point of woodland Stard side
    13 1/2 where we encamped.

Courses & Distances 16th of May 1805
S.80. W. 9 1/2 Miles to a point of wood
    land on the Stard side
S.71. W. 4 1/2 miles to a timbered point on the
    Stard side.
    7

Course & Distance May 15th
S.70. W. 1 1/2 to a wood point on
    the Stard side
S.75. W. 2 to a wood on the Stard side
West 1 1/2 along the Stard side to a point
N.70. W. 2 to a point of wood on the
    Lard side. Hill approach the river
S.80. W. 3 1/2 for the entrance of a timbered creek
    on the Lard side
N.12. W. 2 to a few trees on the Lard side
    West 1 along the Lard side opposite a
    on this Stard side little
    or no timber

Courses & distances of the 17th Continued

S.70. W. 1 1/2 along the Stard land
S.50. W. 1/2 along the Lard side
S.30. W. 1/4 along the Lard side
S.10. W. 1/4 along the Lard side
South 1/4 along the Lard side
S.15. E. 1/2 along the Lard side
N.80. E. 1/2 along the Lard side
S.35. E. 1/2 along the Lard side to the
    commencement of a bluff
    in a bend on Lard
S.2. W. 1/2 to a point of timber Stard
S.45. W. 1/2 to a point of timber Lard
S.20. E. 1/4 to a point of timber Stard
S. 3/4 along the Stard point
S.15 1/2 W. along the Stard point passing
    the entrance of a large creek
    on Lard side
S.80. W. 1 1/2 to a point of woodland Lard
    passing bluffs on Stard side
    here we encamped for
    night.

20 1/2

Courses & Distances 14th of May
S.66. W. 3 1/2 to a point of timber on Stard
    opposite high unknown hills
N.80. W. 1/2 along the Stard side hill
N.45. W. 1 1/2 mile to a point of wood on
    the Lard side opposite
S.80. W. 1 1/2 to a point of timber Lard
S.60. W. 1/2 to a point of timber Stard
    opposite to a bluff
S.85. W. 2 to a point Lard side
S.60. W. 1/2 along the Lard shore
South 1 1/2 to a point of woodland Stard
    opposite to a bluff
S.45. W. 1/2 along the Stard point to the
    extremity of a sand bar opposite
N.20. W. 2 1/2 to a point of woodland on Lard
    the river making a bend to
    the North
N.55. W. 1 to a large tree in the center of
    bend on Stard side
S.70. W. 1 1/4 to the point of a sand bar on Stard
    side passing the entrance of
    a dry creek on Stard
    19 1/4 or 1/2 miles.

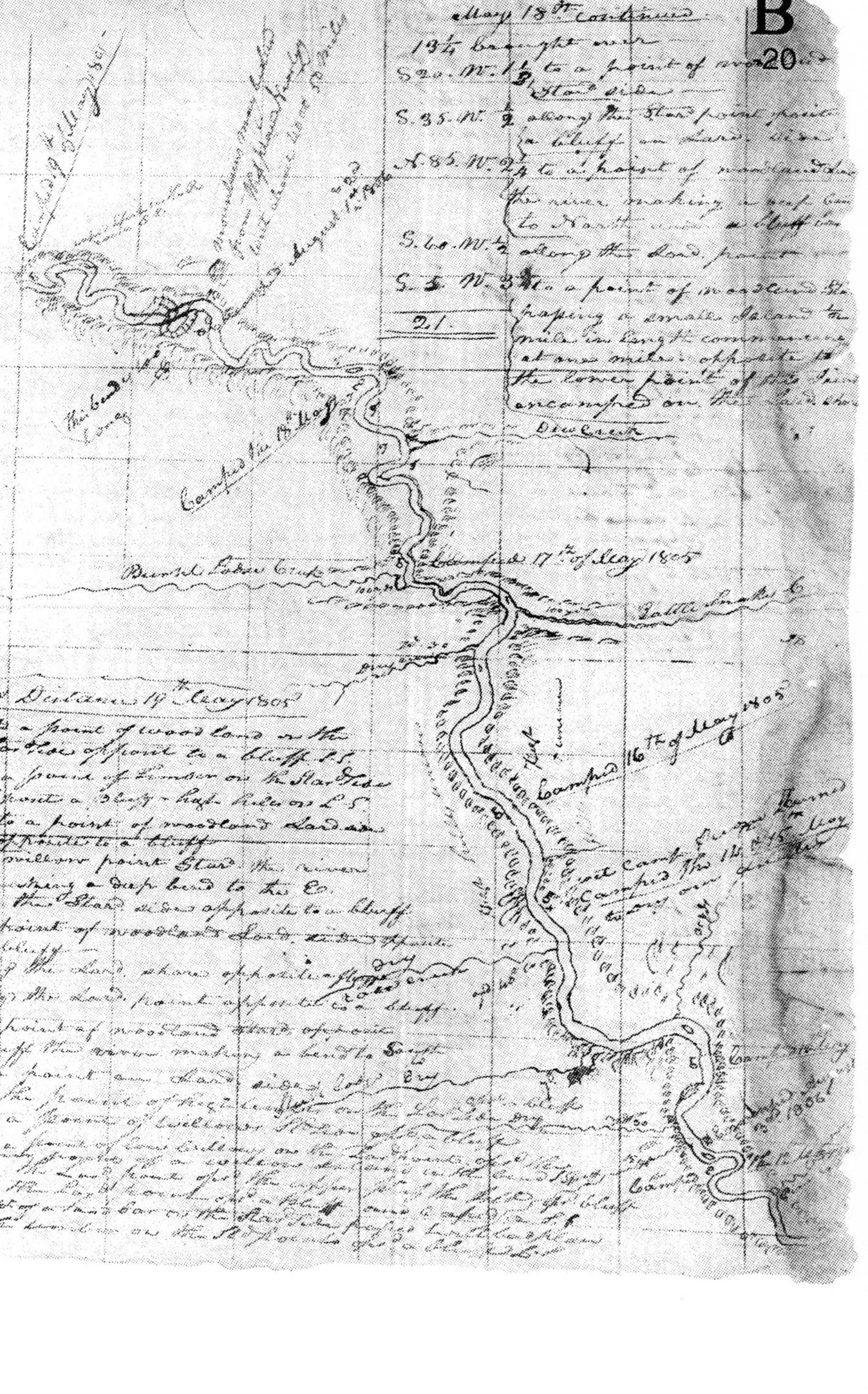

21. The Missouri from below Musselshell River to South Mountain Creek—the route of May 20-24, 1805.

Course & Distance 20th of May 18__

N 70° E 1/_ to a Sand point on the S.d side
N 20° W 1/_ to the timber on the S.d shore
N 10° E 1/4 to the entrance of a Large Creek on the Lard side
... 1/_ to the point of timber on the Lard side opposite to a Bluff S.S.
S 30° E 1/_ to a willow point on Star.d opposite a bluff on Lard side
... 4. along the Star.d point opposite a bluff
... to a point of woodland Lard just below which the ____ river falls in on the Lard side. 100 ___ ___

Course Distance 21st of May 180_

... to a point of timber on S.d side
N 15° W 1/4 along the Star.d point Hill L.d
N 20° E 2. to a point of timber on the Lard S.W. op.d a Bluff Star.d side
N 30° W 1/_ to a point of timber both on the Star.d side op.d to a bluff
N 20° E 1/_ to a point of timber on the Lard S.S op.d a bluff. S.S
N 35° W 1/_ to a point of woodland S.d
N 60° W 1/_ to a point of woodland Star.d
N 15° W 1/_ along the Star.d shore op.d opposite a bluff on Lard side
N 15° E 1/_ to a point of woodland Lard
N 70° W 1. to a point of woodland Star.d
N __ 1/2. along the Star.d shore
S 10° W 1/_ to the extremity of a willow bar on Lard. side.
N 60° W 1/_ to a point of woodland Lard
... 1/_ to the commencement of a bluff in a bend to the N.d S.d coast opposite on the Star.d side
N 75° W 1. to a point of woodland Star.d
N 50° W 2. to a tree in the center of Star.d bed
N 30° W 2. to the lower point of a wood bottom under a bluff in a bend on Star.d side, passing a point on Lard and bluff Star.d where we encamped ___ night

---

Course & Distance May 22d

N 30° E 1/_ the lower point of a Island in a bend of the Lard side
West 1. to the point of timber on the ___ ___ Star.d side pass.d the upp.d p.t of a
West 2. along the Star.d side woodland
S 70° W 3. to a point of wood land on the Star.d side passing under a bluff op.d op.d an Is.d in a bend to the Star.d side
N 45° W 2. to a point of timber on the Lard side
West 1. to the point of a large willow ___ on the Lard side ___ bluff, a Creek ___ on S.S in a deep bend to the Star.d side
South 1/2. to a point of high wood on the Star.d side passing ___ point ___ over a shallow ___ bar S.S of Is.d
S 65° W 1/4 along the Star.d shore opposite to a bluff covered with pine
West 1. to a point of woodland Lard opposite a bluff
S 30° W 2. to a willow point on Star.d side
S 60° W 2 1/4 to a point of woodland Star.d opposite to a bluff where we encamped for the night

16½ Miles.

Course & Distance May 23d

N 85° W 1/_ to the entrance of a Creek in a bend to the Star.d side
S 70° W 1/4 to the point on wood Lard side
S 50° W 1/_ to a point of wood land Star.d
S 50° W 1 1/2 along the Star.d side, a hill opposite on which there is pine
West 2. to a tree in a bend to the Star.d side
N 45° W 2. to the upper point of an Is.d in a bend to the Lard side opposite the center of the Island a small creek falls in on S.d the Island ___ mile in length
S 75° W 1/2 to a point of woodland Star.d side a bluff just above ___ a creek falls in on Lard side
S 85° W 3. to the corner point of a timbered bottom along a bluff in a bend on Star.d passing ___ to the upper point of the timber in the bottom on Lard under a bluff
N 8° W 2. to a point of woodland Star.d opposite a bluff just above ___ a creek falls in on Lard
S 15° W 1 1/2 to a point of woodland Lard opp.d Is.d to a bluff ___ point
West 1/2 along the Lard ___ point
17½ ½

Course and distance May 23rd continued

distance brought over 14½ Miles

N 60 W 1 to a point of timbered land Stard
N 65 W 2 to a point of timbered land Stard
passing a small Island in a deep
bend to the N bluff on Stard
opposite the Island

S 65 E 2½ to a point of woodland Stard
opposite to a bluff

N 75 W 4 to the upper part of a bluff
N 80 E 1½ in a bend on Lard side
to the upper point of a small
Island in a bend below to N E

S E ¾ along the Lard shore to
the point of a woodland Lard

S 45 W 1½ to a point of wood in a bend
on Lard under a hill
opposite to which we are
camped on Stard side —

27 S

Course & distance 24th May 1804

N 6 W 1½ to the mouth of Wood River in a bend Stard 5°
N 60 W ½ to a point of wood Stard side of a bluff Lard
S W ¾ along the Stard shore past a bluffs Lard
N 60 W 1½ along the Stard side to Accord may
the timber under a bluff — in about 1
a creek falling in on Stard side
village of Barton & Sprads on Stard
N W ¾ to a point on the Lard side Lard side
N 70 W 2½ to a grove of trees with timber on Lard
to the bluff we passed a Island on S Lard
S W 1 to a point of woodland Stard side
S 50 W 1½ to a point of woodland Stard side opposite
a low bluff and high pinnacles —
W 2½ to the lower point of the timber on a
bend on Lard passing a Stard point at 1½ m
Stard being opposite the lower point of a small
Island

N 60 W 2¼ to the lower point of the timber on a Stard
bend passing the island at ½ mile a small
creek falling in on Stard at the
extremity of the creek opposite the
lower point of a small island

S W 1¼ along the Stard shore to
a bluff in a bend Lard passing
the Island at ¾ m and a Stard point

S 80 W 1¼ to a point of woodland Stard
passing bluff on Lard

W 3 to the point of a high bluff Mile Rock
N 78 W ¾ in a bend on Lard a large stream
falling in just below the bluff on Lard
N W 1 to a Stard point
S W 1 to a point of wood Stard
Stard side —

From the Junction of the Shell River to the opposite side of Missouri is N. 46° W. From the point up the Missouri is S. 12° W. 64 poles to a tree from the said tree across the Missouri is N. 31 ½° E

From the Point across the Shell River to a Stake is S. 24° E from the point up the Shell River is S. 13° W. 38 poles to a tree from the said tree across the shell river to the stake is N. 75½° E

Shell River

222 yards

110 yards

2270 wid

Missouri

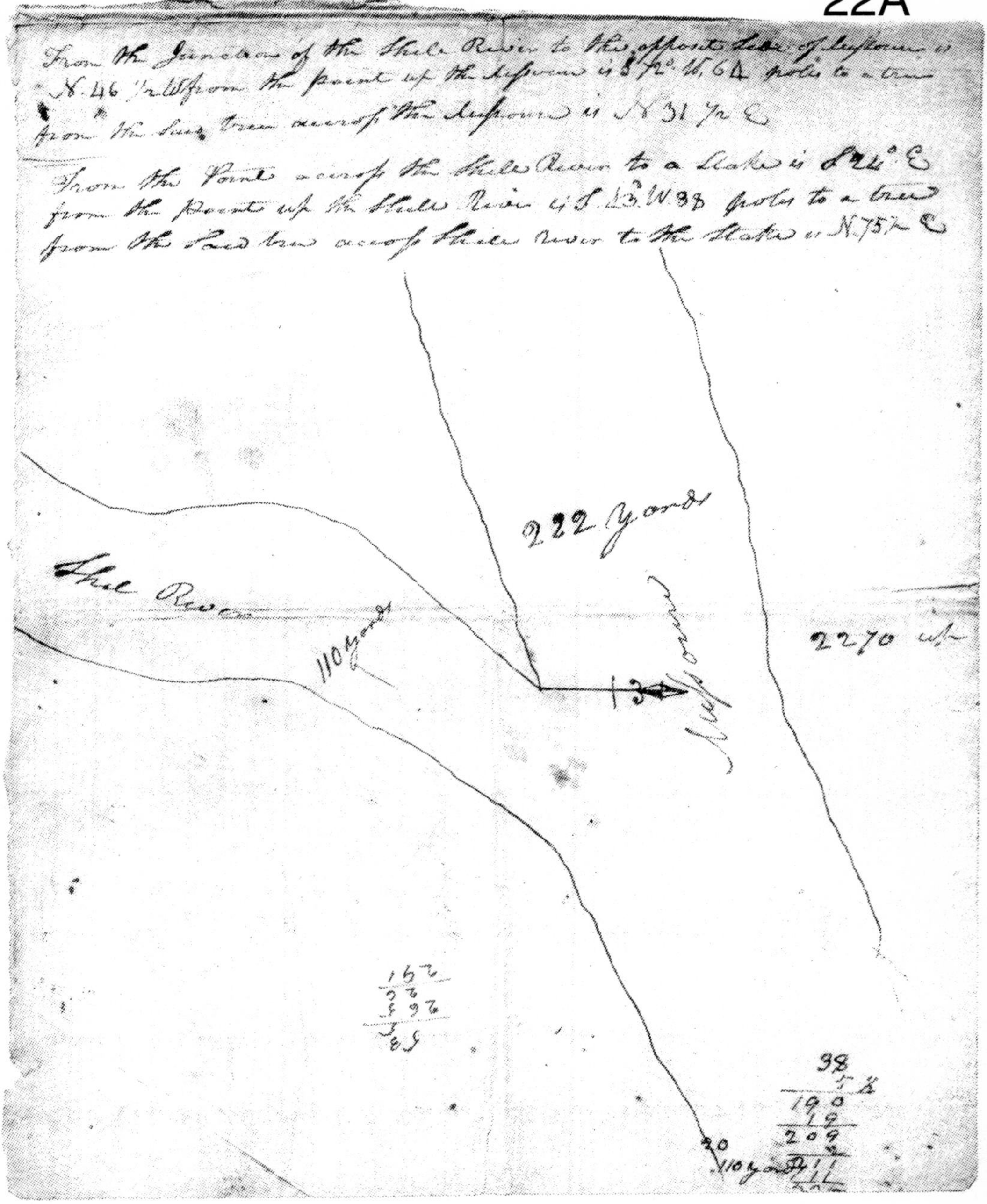

22A.   Junction of the (Mussel)shell and the Missouri, May 20, 1805.

23. The Missouri from South Mountain Creek to Judith's River—the route of May 24-28 ; with return camps also marked, in July, 1806.

Courses and distances of the 28th May

Continued

Distance brought forward, 20 ½

N. 64° W. ¼ to the upper part of the timber on a timbered bottom on Stard. where we encamped for the night

Miles — 21 ½

Course 2d Division May 29th

S. 65° W. 2 ½ to a ...

S. 80° W. 1 to the ...

S. 50° W. 2 to a tree in the Stard. ...

South 1 to a tree on the Stard. ...

S. 88° W. 2 ½ to the upper ...

S. 75° W. 2 to a few trees on ...

N. 70° W. 1 ½ to a ...

N. 86° W. ¾ on the Lard. side ...

S. 70° W. 1 to a ...

West 1 ¾ to a few trees on ...

S. 72° W. 1 ½ to a few trees on the ...

S. 85° W. 1 ½ to a bluff point on Stard. opposite the mouth of a river

West — ... along the ... bluff

N. 85° W. ¾ to a point of woodland Stard.

Miles 18

Camps May 28th 1805

Camped 27th of May

60 m from 26th May

Camp 26th of May 1805

Camps May 25th 1805

course July 30th 1806

Camp 23rd May

Camp 24th of May 1805

South Mountain

Course & Distance at N W 25 ...

S 50° W 2 ¾ to the entrance of a ... Creek
in a bend to the Lard Side ...
passing a small Island in a ...
bend to the Lard Side a ...

N 57° W 1 ¾ to the Star dew of an Island ...
from the S. Shore by a Channel ...
a Bluff on the L. Side

N 35° W ¾ on the S. Side passed a Sand b. d
N 15° W ½ to a point of woodland Lard
N 30° W 2 to a point of woodland Star'd
opposite the Lower point of an
Island

S 25° W ½ to a bluff bank, in the Star'd bend
opposite ... of the Island

N 65° W 9 ½ to a bluff point on Star'd
opposite the upper point of
the Island

N 60° W 4 to a clump of trees in a Star'd
bend under a high bluff
passing a Sand point at ¼ m.
and a small Island at ½ Miles

N 56° W 1 to the point of a high plain on Star'd
passing an Island ... the
Stard above ¾ of a mile in length

S 80° W 2 to the Lower point of a wooded
Island in the middle of the river passed
the point on the Lard Side at ...

N 60° W 1 to a point on the Lard Side passed
the head of the Island at ...
miles 18   Camped Lard Side

Courses and distances 21st of May 1805

S 45° W 1 to the point of a plain on Star'd
opposite a bluff

N 00° W ½ along the Star'd point opp.t bluff
N 45° W ½ along the Star'd point opp.t a bluff
N 40° W ½ along the Star'd point opposite a bluff
N 30° E 4 along the Star'd point opp.t high hills
N 85° E 2 to a timbered point on Lard side
N 10° W ¾ to a point in a bend on Star'd
N 75° W ½ to a point of timber on Star'd
N 66° W 1 to a point of timber Lard side
N 18° W 1 to a point of grass on Lard side
N 12° E 1 to the mouth of a creek Star'd side
West 3 ½ to some trees on the Lard point
S W ¼ 1 ½ to some timber in a bend L.d S.d
N 80° W ½ to open prairie on the Lard
N 60° W 1 ... on the Lard Side
13   course forward

May 26th brought forward
13   ... no timber on the banks of
river on either Side Bluffs
much bark & sharol ...

S 24° W 2 to a clif in a bend to the Lard Sid
West 2 to a point on the Lard Sid
timber on either bank

S 60° W ½ to a ... bluff point ...
opposite the upper point of
... sand Island

S 45° W 4 to the point of a small Island
passing high bluffs on both
Sides

S 70° W 1 to the point of a high bluff
in a Star'd bend

N 80° W 4 to the upper point of a tim
bered bottom on Lard side
where we encamped for
the night

22 ¾

Courses and distances May 27 18
West 1 3 ½ along the Lard shore to
a point on Star'd no land
bluffs approach the river on
both sides

S 80° W ¾ to a bluff point Star'd side
in a Star'd bend

S 55° W 1 to a Lard point

S 8° W 1 ½ to the point of a bluff
on Star'd in ... bend
river narrowing ... to
bend to S. B.

S 60° W ½ to a open point on Lar'd
S 20° W 1 ½ to a single cotton tree Star'd
S 15° W 1 to a bluff point on the Lar'd
S 15° W 5 to a bluff point on the ...
19 ½ depend Lard pt ... ...

Courses and Distances May
Miles
South ½ to a point on the ...

S 35° W 2 ... from the bluff
to the point of a bluff Star'd

S 60° W 1 ½ to a point on Star'd
N 70° W 1 to a point on Lar'd
S 65° W 2 to a point on Star'd
N 65° W 1 ½ to a single cotton tree on Star'd
West 1 ½ to cotton tree on Lar'd
N 82° W ½ to a grove of cotton trees L.d
N 76° W 2 to a tree on the Lard point
S 68° W 2 to a point on Star'd side
West 2 ½ to the upper part of a bluff
bottom in a bend on the Star'd
passing ... in a ...

S 20° W 2 ½ to a bluff point in a ...
... Side passed two small ...

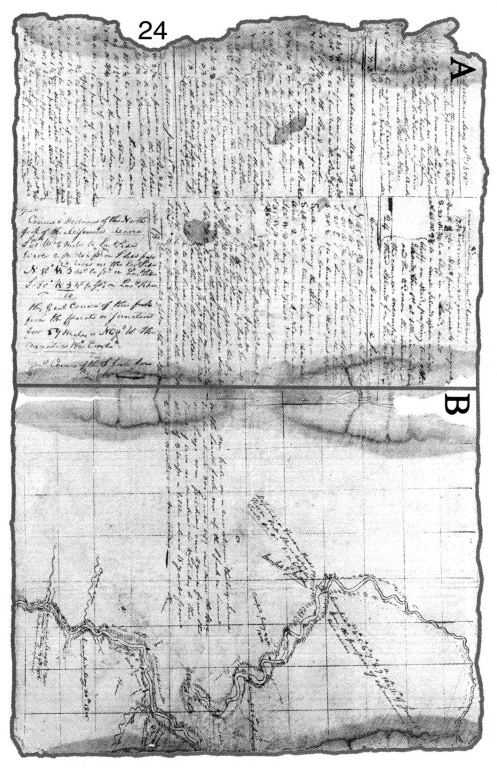

24. The Missouri from Judith's River to Maria's River, showing also the course of the latter, and camping places for May 29-June 11, 1805 ; with indications of camping places in July, 1806.

A
-24

[illegible] & Distances May 30th 1805

[illegible] W.	¾	along the timbered bottom on the Lard point, a high bluff opst.
[illegible] 50° W.	2	to a few trees on the Lard. point
[illegible] 60° W.	2	to a Stump on the Stard. point opst. a high black bluff
[illegible] 70° W.	½	on the Stard. shore to a few trees
[illegible] W.	[illegible]	[illegible] the mouth of a small Creek [illegible] a [illegible] on the Stard. Side
[illegible] 55° W.	2½	to a grove of trees in a bend to the Lard. Side passed a Small Island at ½ mile
Miles	8½	

Courses and Distances May 31st 1805

N. 45° W.	2	to a few trees in a bend Stard. S.
[illegible] 30° W.	½	to a few trees on the Stard. point
[illegible] 35° W.	¾	on the Stard. point
[illegible] 60° W.	1¾	to the lower point of a timber in a Stard. Bend
[illegible]	¾	to a few trees on the Stard. Side
[illegible] 75° W.	2	on the Stard. Side to some trees
[illegible]	2	on the [illegible] the [illegible] point
[illegible]	[illegible]	on the Stard. point
[illegible] 45° W.	¾	on the Stard. point opst. a high
[illegible]	¾	[illegible] [illegible] from the [illegible]
South	1½	to a tree in the bend the Stard. Side opposite a high [illegible] bottom
[illegible] 22° W.	1	to the point on the Stard. Side
[illegible] 15° E.	3½	to a point on the Lard. Side, a high black Conical [illegible] about 100 feet
[illegible] 20° W.	2½	to a tree in a bend to the Lard.
[illegible]	2½	to a Small timbered bottom above the mouth of a Creek on the Stard. Side [illegible] a high [illegible] [illegible] encamped on [illegible]
	18	

[illegible] and Distances June 1st 1805

[illegible] W.	2½	to a point on the Stard. Side
[illegible] W.	1½	to a point on the Lard. Side
[illegible] W.	1½	to a point on the Stard. Side
[illegible] W.	1½	to a tree on the Lard. Side
[illegible] 25 W.	1¼	to a point on Stard. Side
[illegible] 30. W.	3/4	along the Stard. shore to a point of woodland
[illegible] 20. W.	1	to a point of timbered land Lard. opposite to a bluff Stard.
[illegible] W.	¾	to a point of timbered land Stard.
[illegible] 32 W.	1½	to a point of timbered land Lard.
[illegible] 60 W.	1¾	to the point of a bluff in a bend on Stard. opposite to a small island
S. [illegible] W.	1½	to a point on Stard. Side
[illegible] 60 W.	1	to the upper point of a small Island, passing the island [illegible] at ¾
[illegible] 40. W.	¾	to a bluff point in a bend on Lard.
West	1	to the [illegible] of a Stard. bend

Courses and distances June 1st Continued

Miles 17¾		distance brought forward.
South	2½	to a Stard. point opposite a [illegible]
S. 20. W.	¾	to a bluff in a Stard. bend
N. 65 W.	2¼	to a small Island opposite a high bluff on Stard., passing two other Islands, the 1st at 1 M. in Lard. [illegible] and the 2nd near the extremity of this course. encamped on the third Island for the night
	24	

Course and Distance 2 June

N. 25° W.	¾	to a few trees on the Lard. [illegible]
S. 60° W.	½	along the Lard. point
S. 40° W.	½	to some trees on the Lard. [illegible]
S. 20° E.	1	to some willows on the Lard. [illegible]
S. 30° E.	1	to a bush on a Stard. point opposite a low bluff
South	¼	along the Stard. point
S. 45 W.	½	to a tree in a bend on Lard. side
West	2	to a point [illegible] [illegible]
S. 68° W.	¼	along the Lard. point & [illegible]
S. 35° W.	½	on the Lard. Side
S. 26 W.	1	to a point of timbered bottom [illegible] the Lard. Side
South	2¾	to a point Stard. Side opst. a [illegible] passing 2 Small Islands
S. 60° W.	1	on the Stard. Side, passed 2 Islands on the Lard. Side
N. 80° W.	1¾	to Lard. point opposite a bluff
S. 10 W.	[illegible]	to the lower point of an island near the Stard. point
S. 62° W.	[illegible]	to a point of timber on the Lard. opposite a bluff passing the Island and one other near the Stard. Side
S. 20° W.	[illegible]	to the head of an Island
South	½	to a point of timber on the [illegible]
S. 10 W.	[illegible]	to a point between two [illegible] where encamped opst. on the Lard. Side
Miles	18	

Courses & Distances of the North [illegible] [illegible] Course
[illegible] 45 W. 2 Miles to Lar. Side
N. 15 W. 2 Miles to a [illegible] on Star. Side
[illegible] Miles to a [illegible] on the Lar. Side
S. 50 W. 3 Miles [illegible] on Lar. Side
N. 80 W. 3 Miles [illegible] on Lar. Side
12
The Great Course of this fork from the point of junction [illegible] 59 Miles N. 62° W. the [illegible] [illegible]
[illegible] Course of the South fork [illegible]

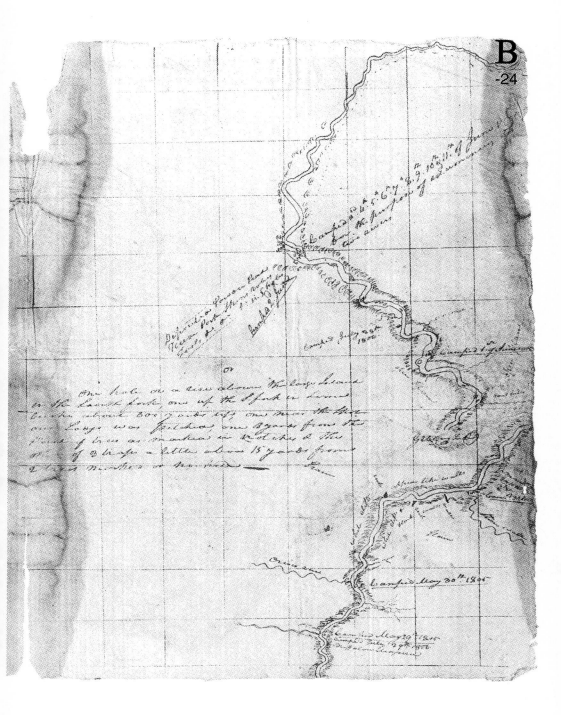

25.　The Missouri from the entrance of Maria's River to the Great Falls, showing camping places for June 11-29, 1805.

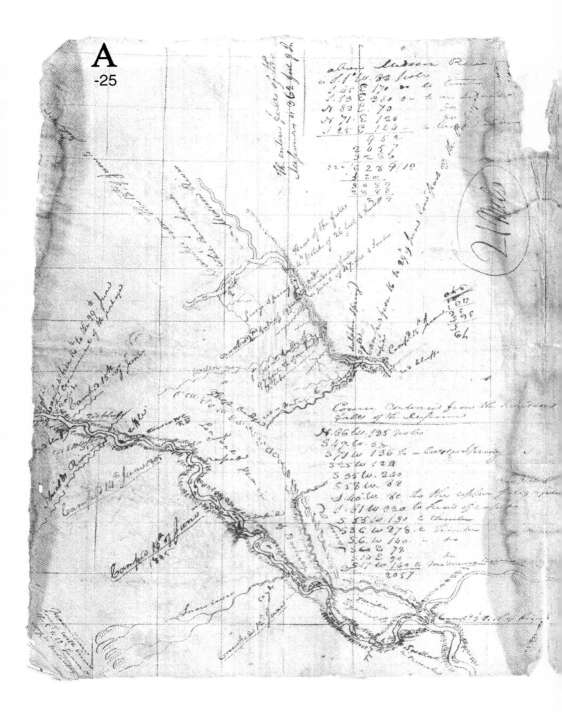

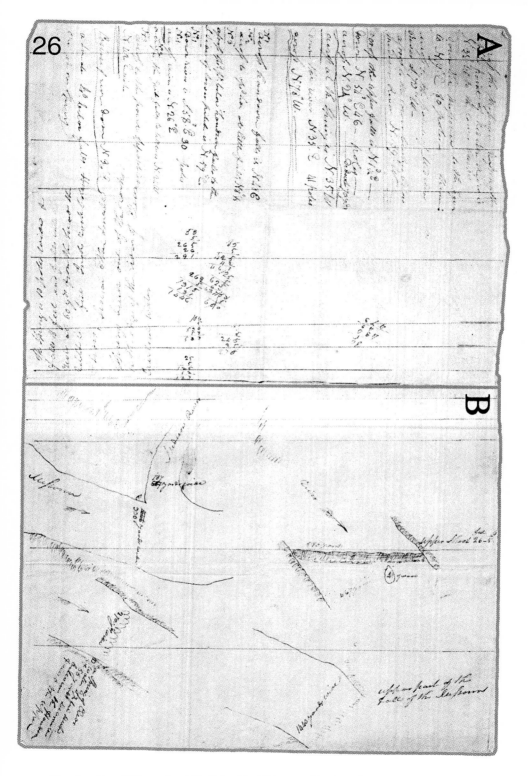

26. Junction of Missouri and Medicine (Sun) Rivers. Sketches of upper parts of Falls and of Giant Spring, or "Large fountain."

of the Mississippi the length
of the point of Madison opposite is
S 35 W to the lower works

Down the Mississippi to the upper
is N 49 E 80 poles ———
across to the point of Madison
below S 73 W —

along the lower boundary above
the lower River N 59 W

across the upper falls is N 1½ E —
down N 54 E 46 — poles
across N 24° W —— deduct 70 yd

across at the Spring is N 35 W

down the river N 35 E 41 poles

across N 78 W. —————

No 1 across handsom falls is N 48 E
No 2 across to opposite at little falls N 8 W
No 3
across 1st St. below handsom falls to the
S side of lower pitch is N 59 E

No 1
Down river to S 58 E 30 poles
No 1
across river to N 26 E

across the great falls to below N 21 W

No 2
across to the point opposite
N 22 W

Course from run down N 35 E

a little W. below falls

one at our Spring

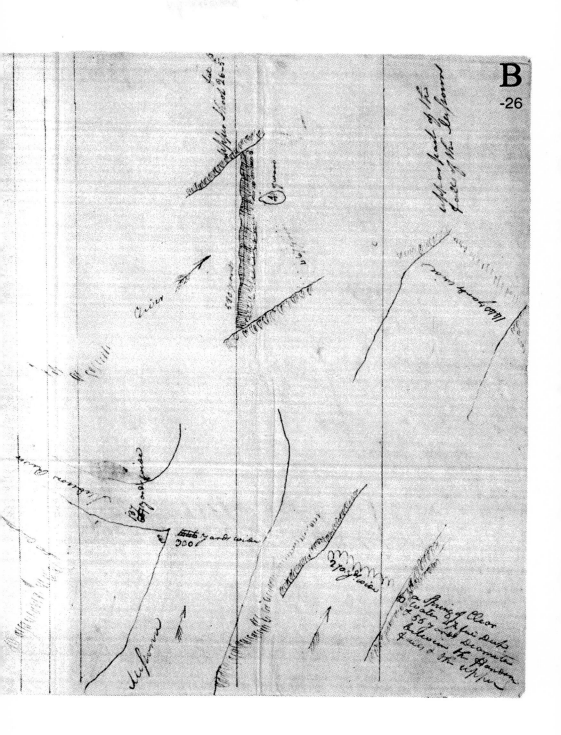

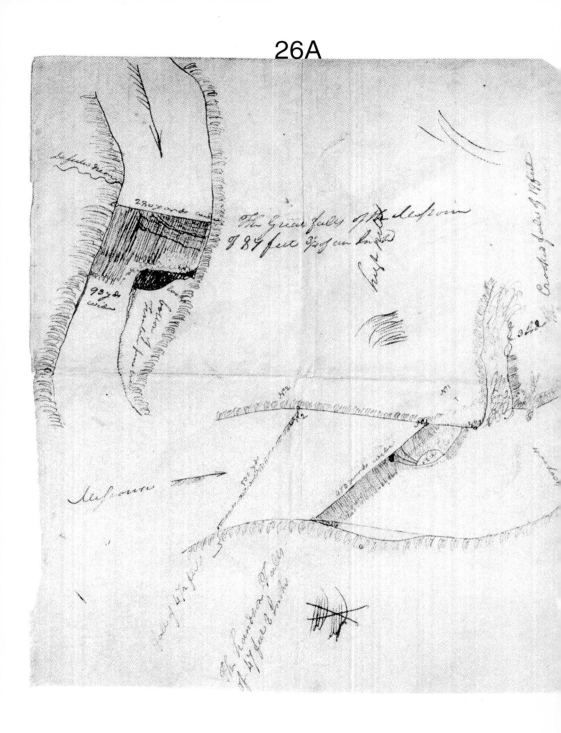

26A.   Sketches of Great, Handsome, and Crooked Falls.

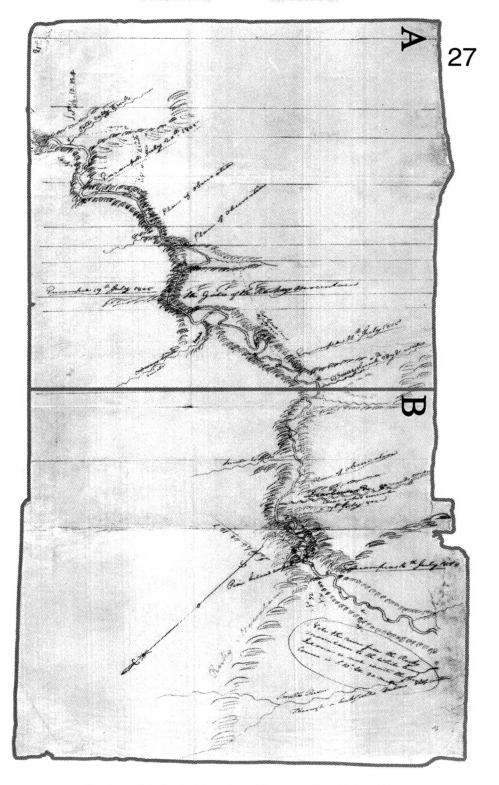

27 . Gates of the Rocky Mountains, with camps of July 16-20, 1805.

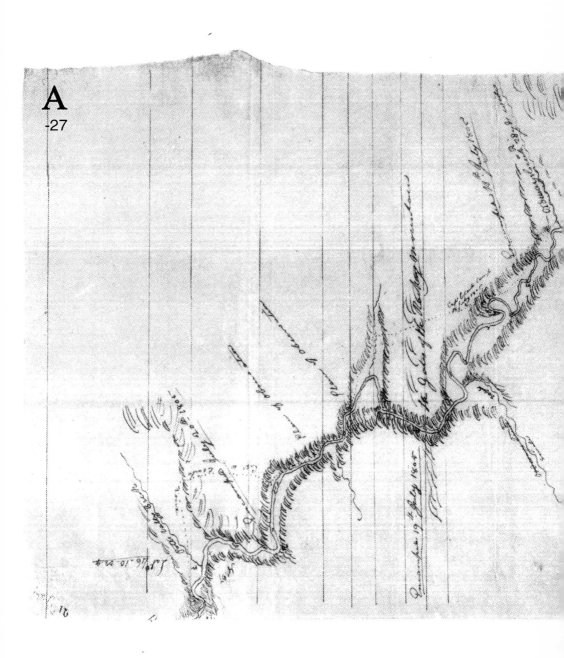

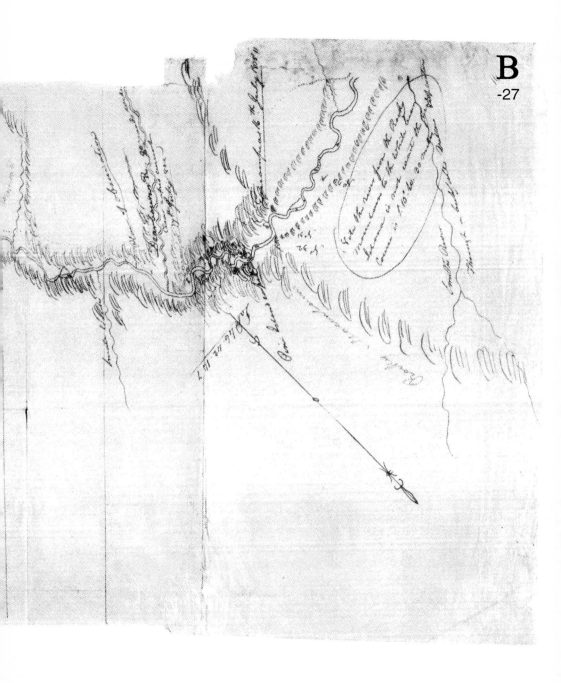

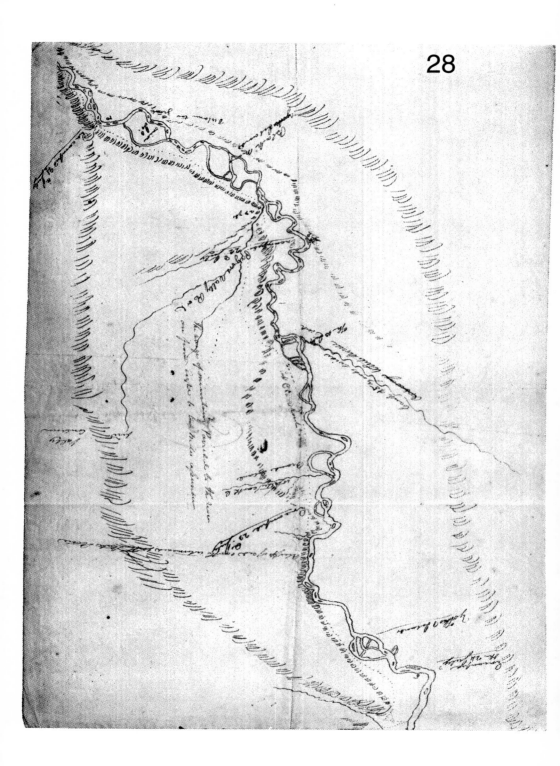

28. Missouri River, giving the route of July 21-24—continuing map No. 27.

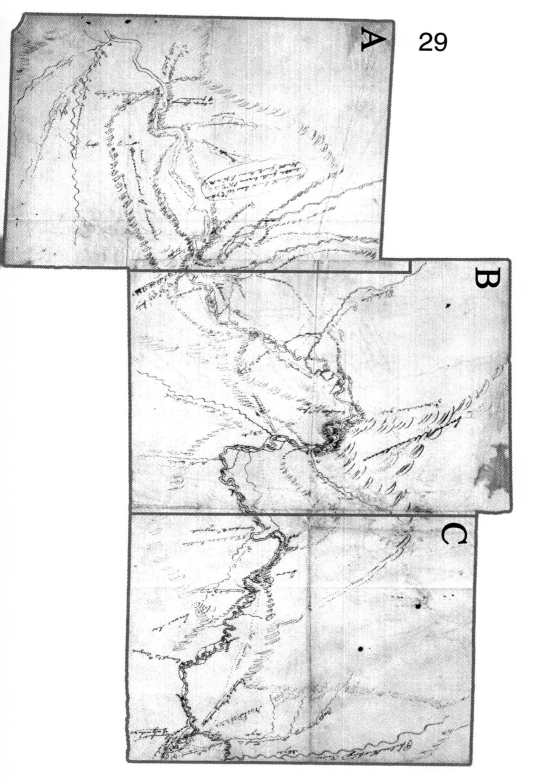

29. Missouri River from Gass's (Hot Springs) Creek to Three Forks ; and Jefferson River to Philanthropy (Stinking Water) River---route of July 25-August 7, 1805.

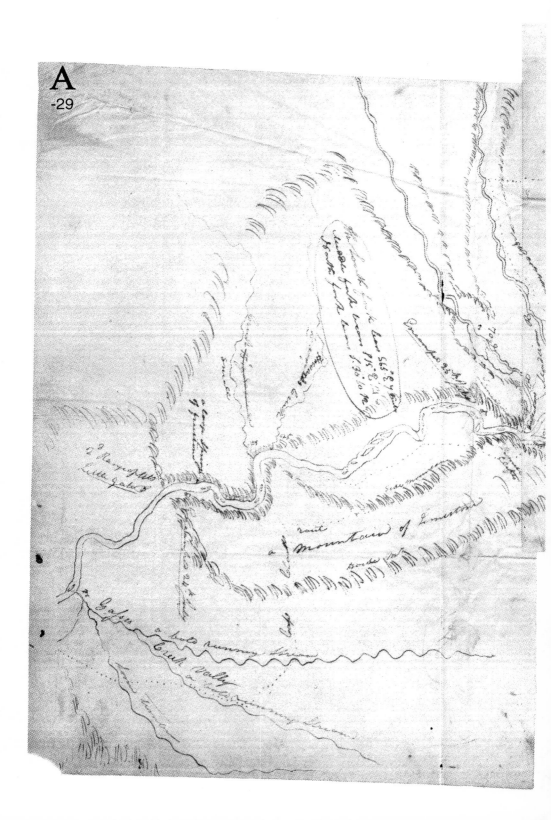

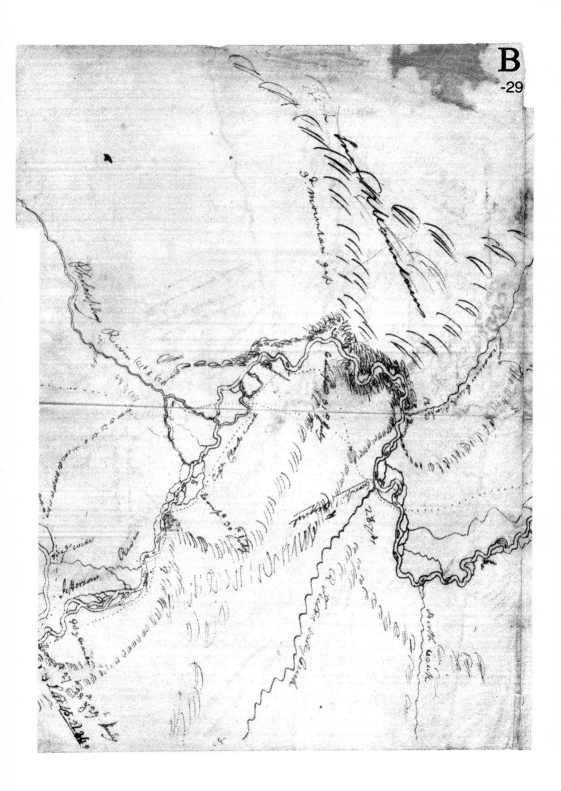

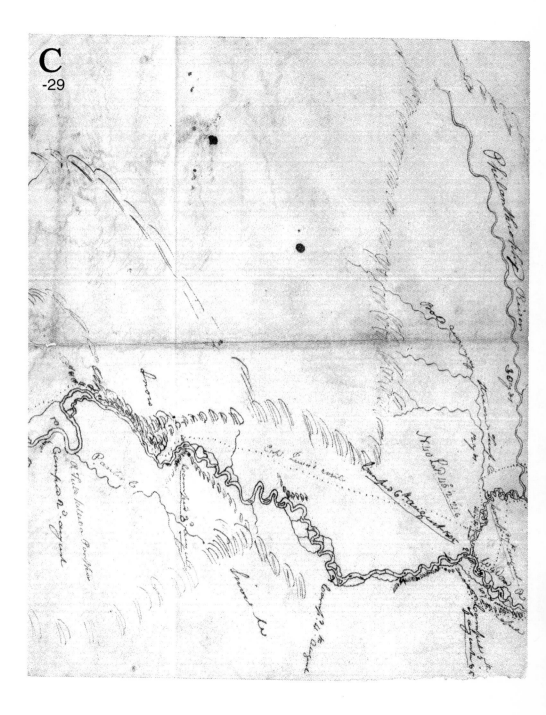

29A

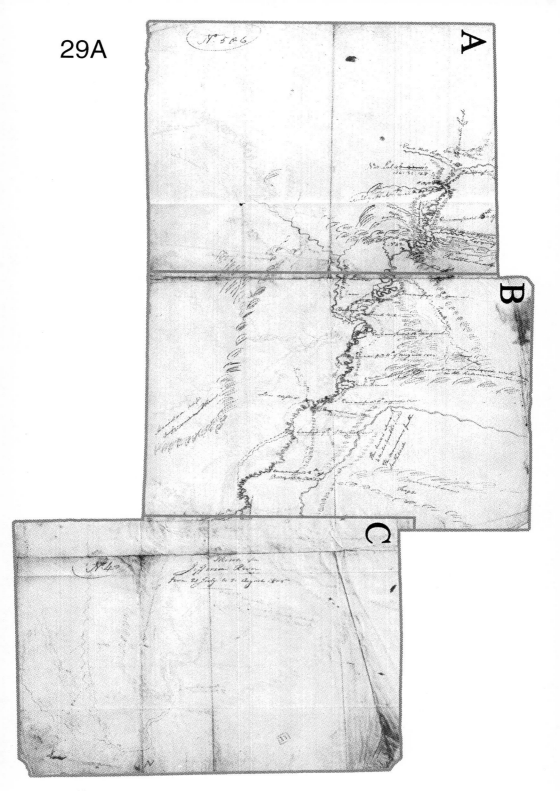

29A. Jefferson River from Philanthropy to the Forks—the route of August 8-20, 1805.

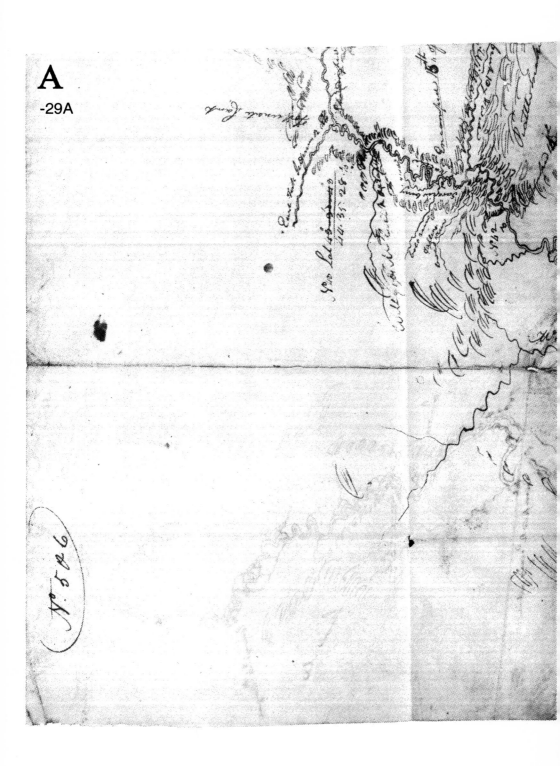

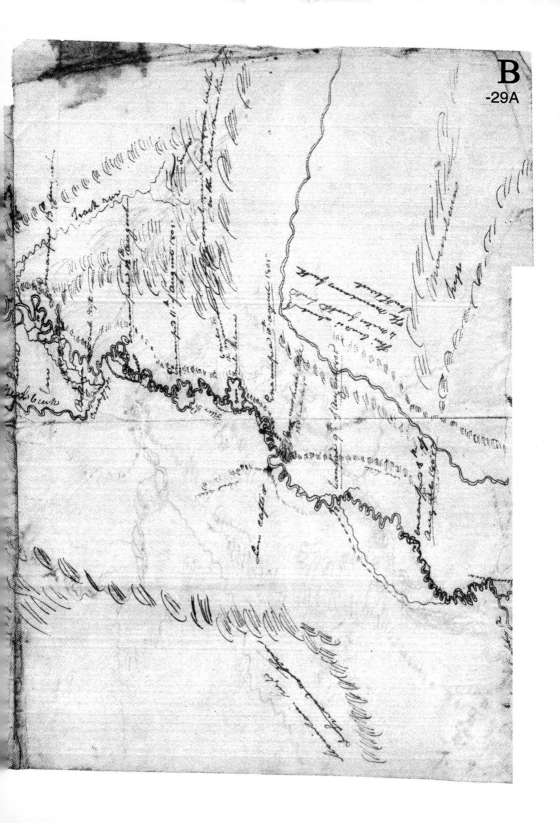

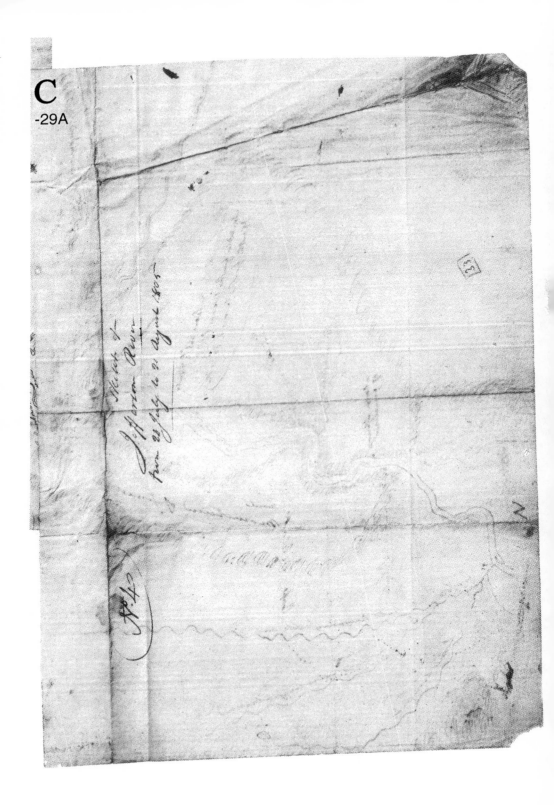

Sketch of
J. Warm River
from 25 July to 2. August 1805

33

N

N° 4

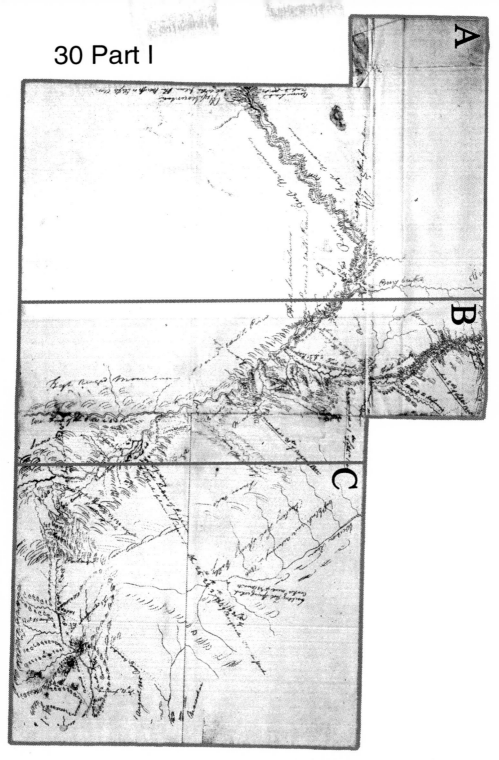

30. "From Jeffersons River to the Forks of Kooskooske over the Rocky Mountains from the 25th of August to the 9th of October, 1805."
This map is of especial importance, as showing the route over the divide, heretofore in doubt.
Part I.

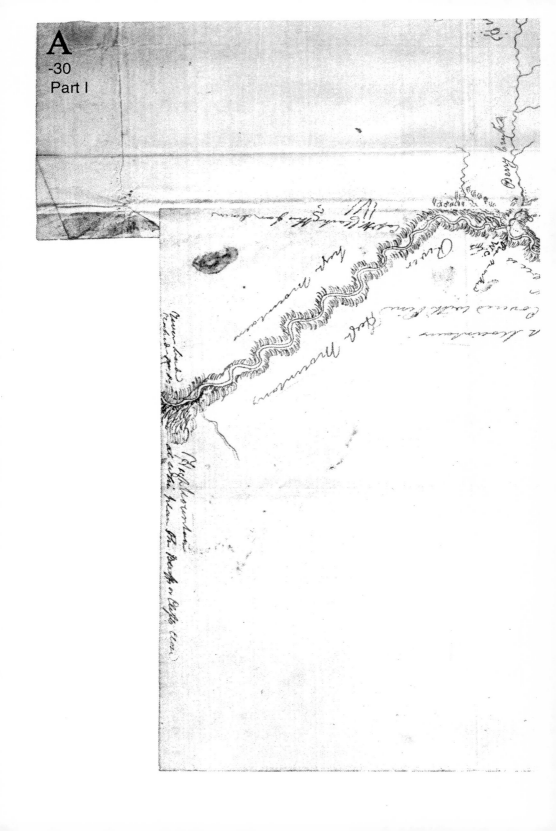

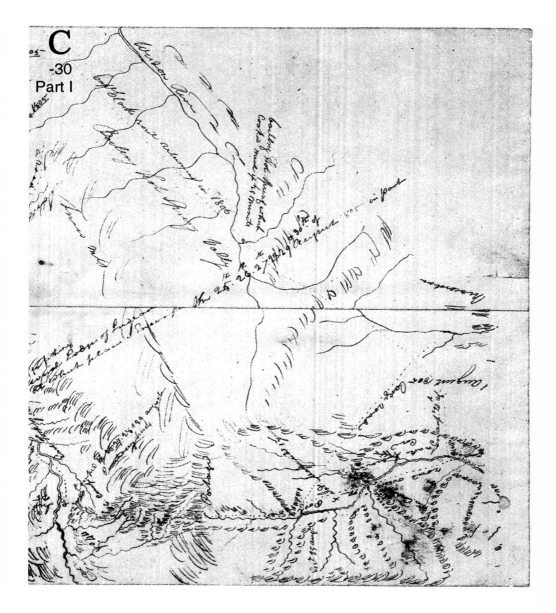

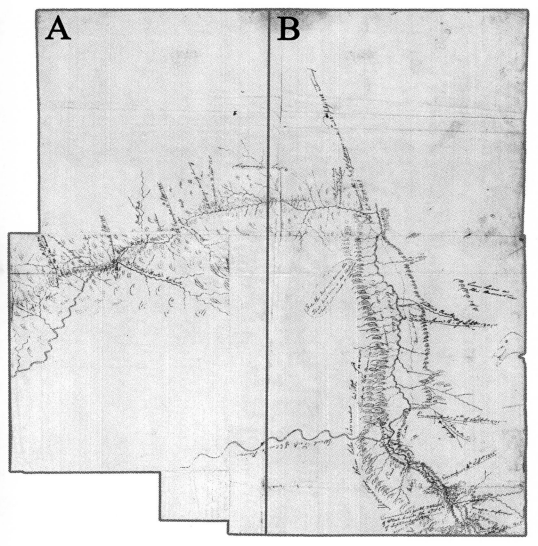

30. "From Jeffersons River to the Forks of Kooskooske over the Rocky Mountains from the 25th of August to the 9th of October, 1805."
This map is of especial importance, as showing the route over the divide, heretofore in doubt.
Part II.

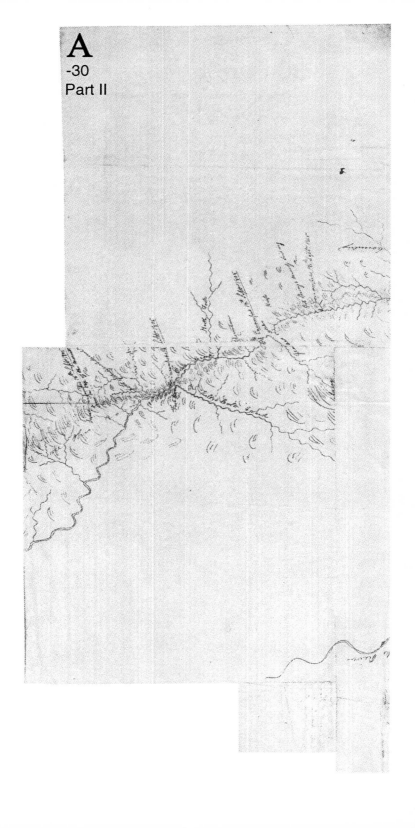

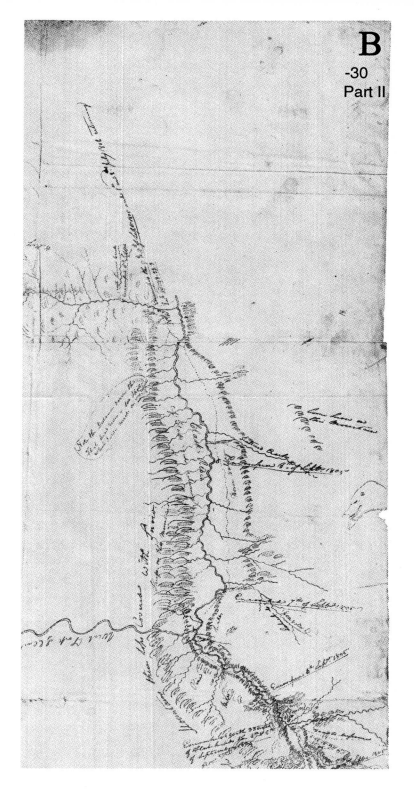

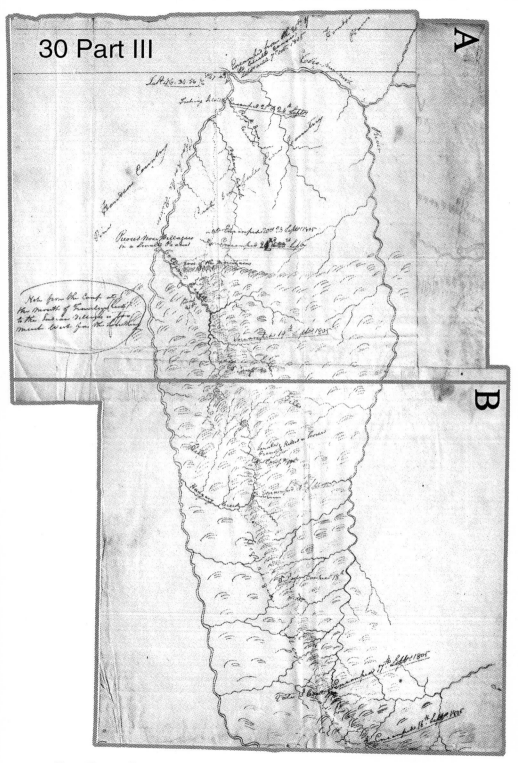

30. "From Jeffersons River to the Forks of Kooskooske over the Rocky Mountains from the 25th of August to the 9th of October, 1805."

This map is of especial importance, as showing the route over the divide, heretofore in doubt.

Part III

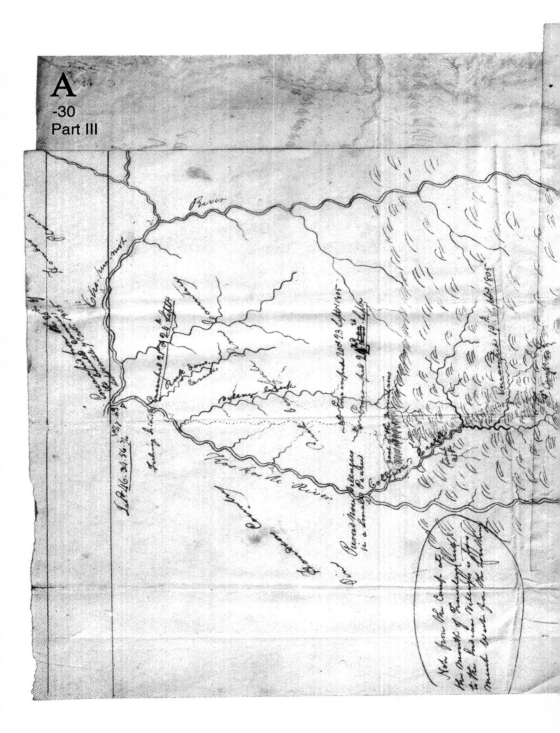

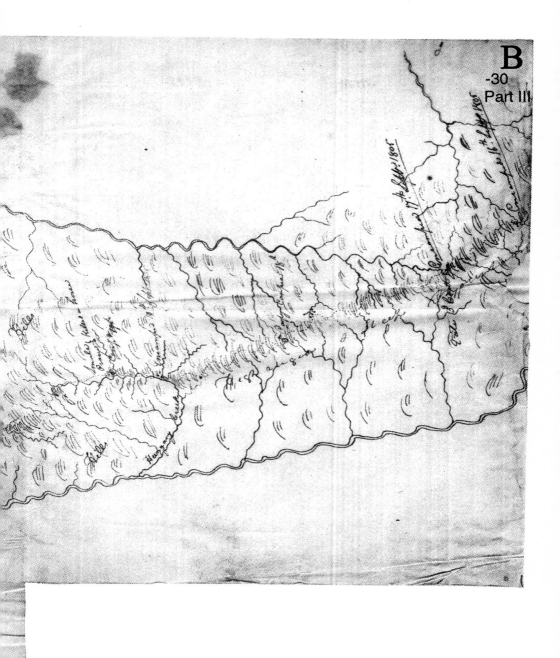

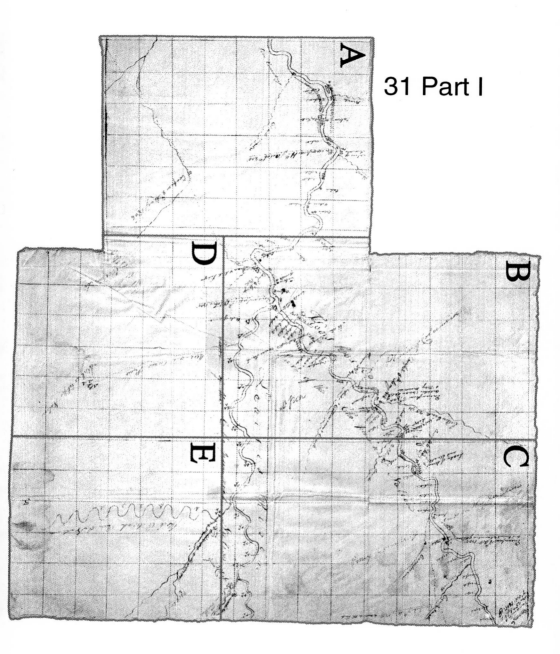

31 Part I

31.   The Kooskooskee, Lewis's (Snake), and upper reaches of Columbia rivers, showing route
from the launching of canoes October 7-October 19, 1805.
Part I.

A

-31

Part I

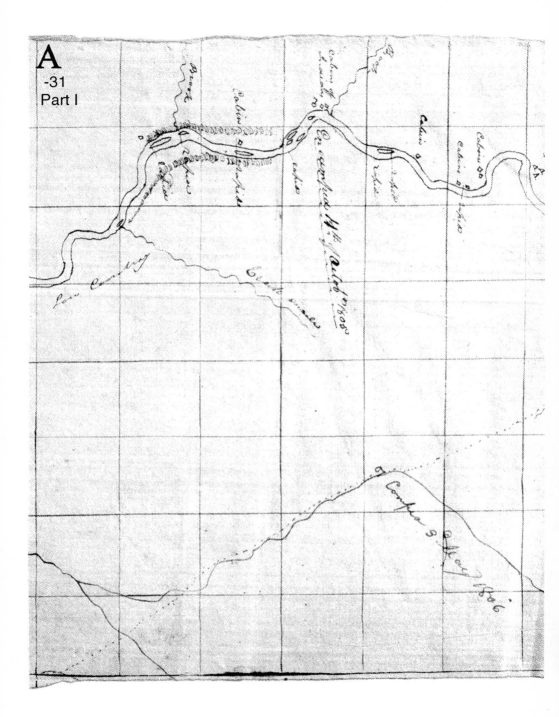

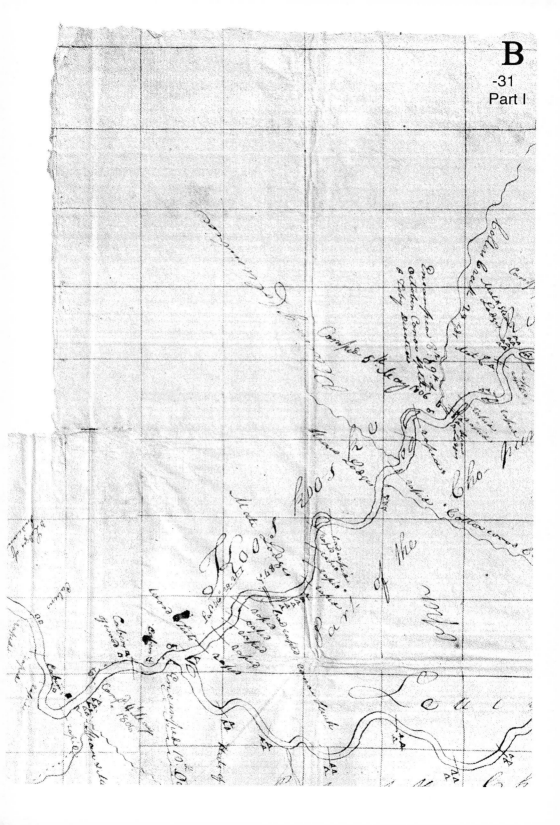

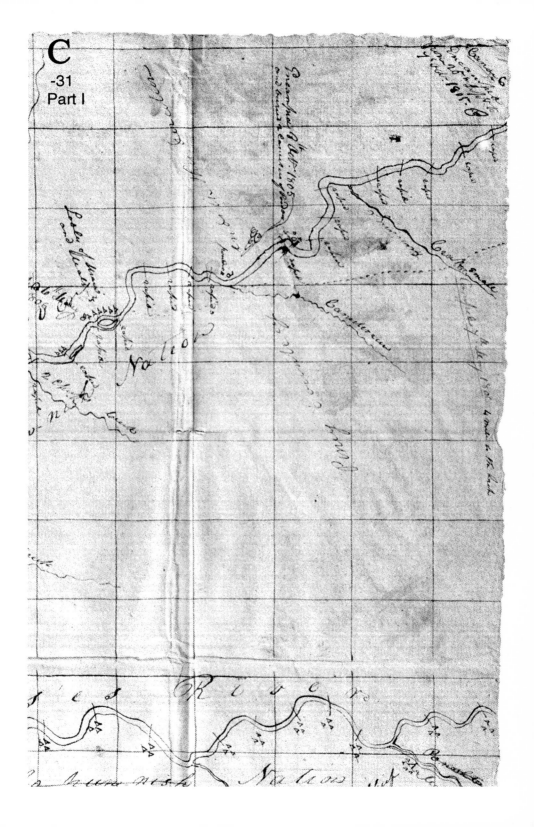

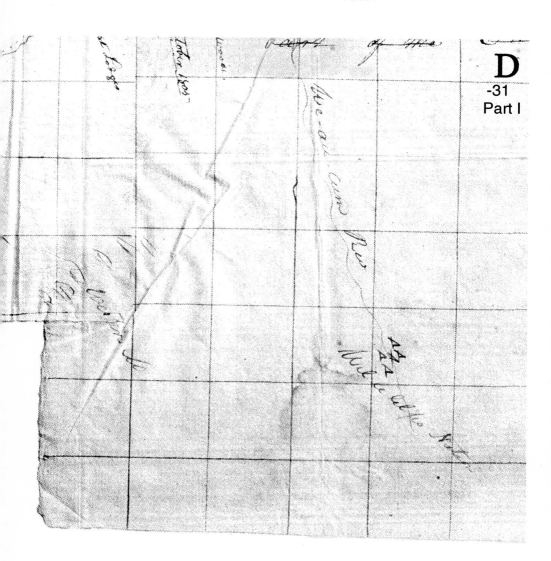

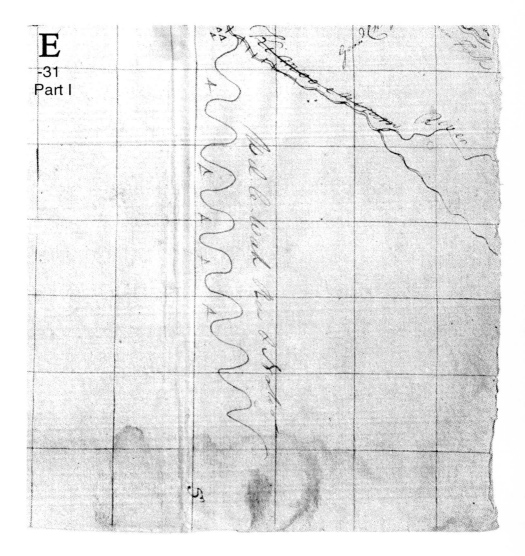

31 Part II

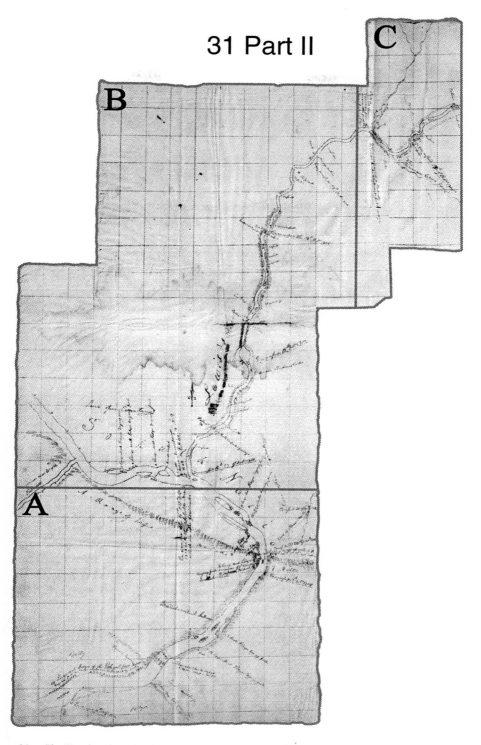

31. The Kooskooskee, Lewis's (Snake), and upper reaches of Columbia rivers, showing route
from the launching of canoes October 7-October 19, 1805.
Part II.

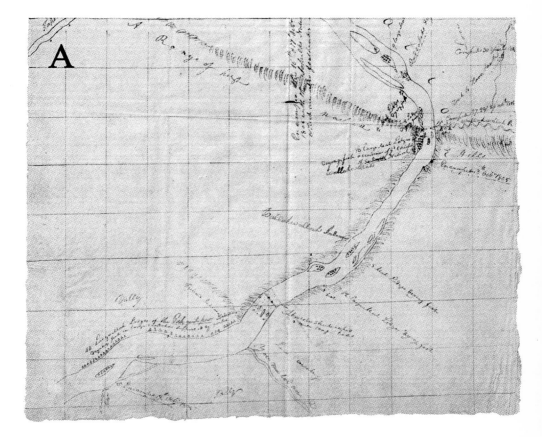

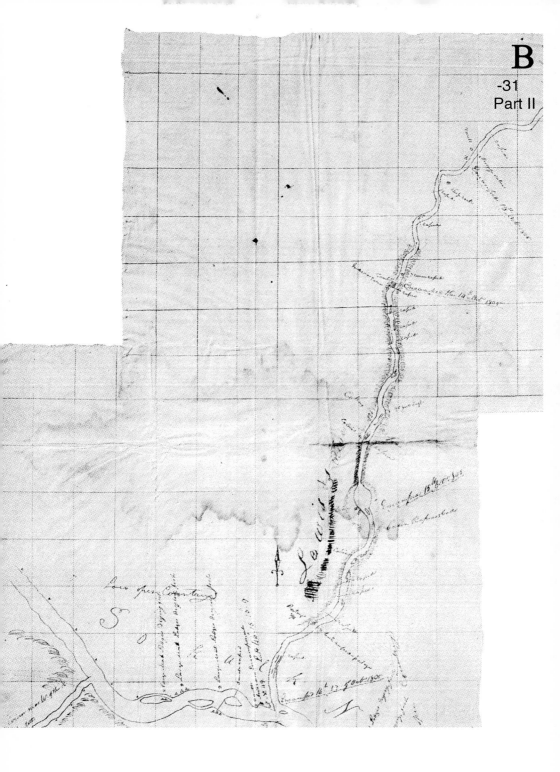

C
-32
Part II

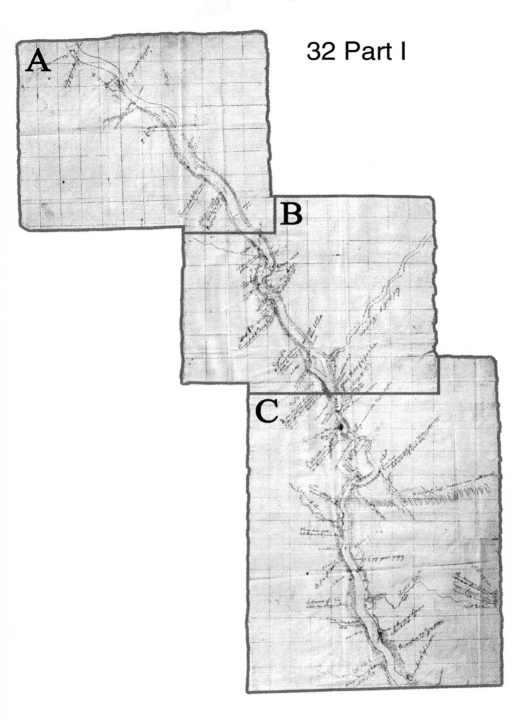

32 Part I

32.   " Sketch of the Columbia River from the forks, & the 19th of October 1805 to the
1st of Jany on the Pacific Ocean."   The map also indicates camping
places on the return journey, in April, 1806.
Part I.

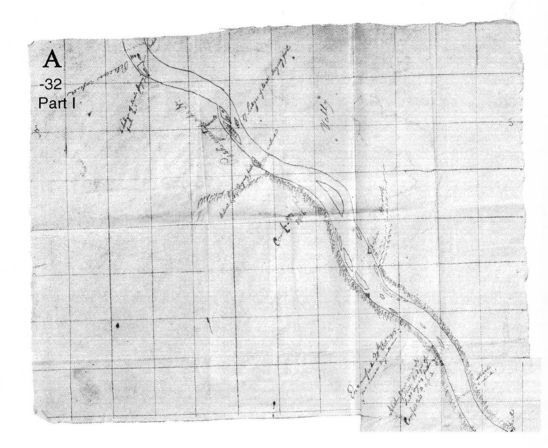

A
-32
Part I

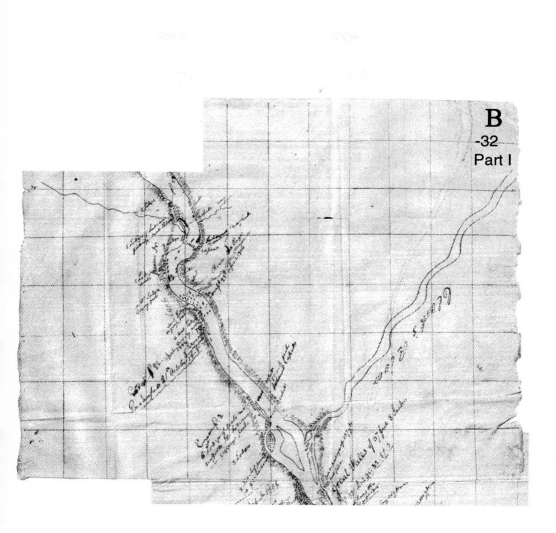

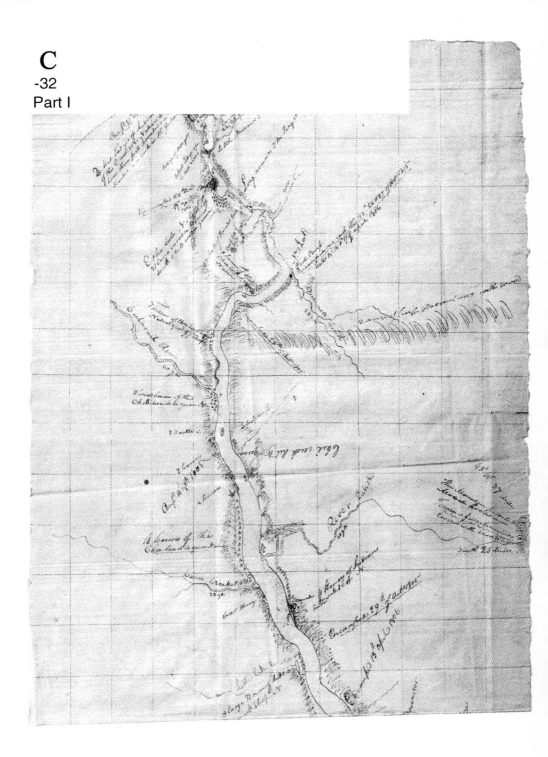

32 Part II

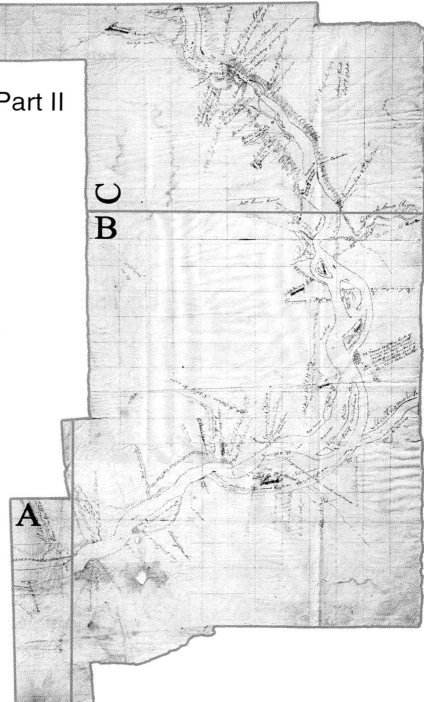

32. "Sketch of the Columbia River from the forks, & the 19th of October 1805 to the
1st of Jany on the Pacific Ocean."   The map also indicates camping
places on the return journey, in April, 1806.
Part II.

A
-32
Part II

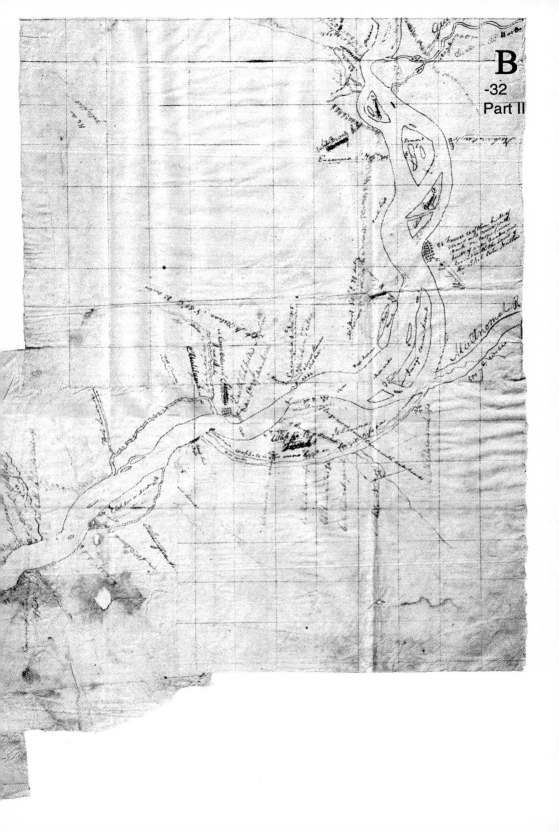

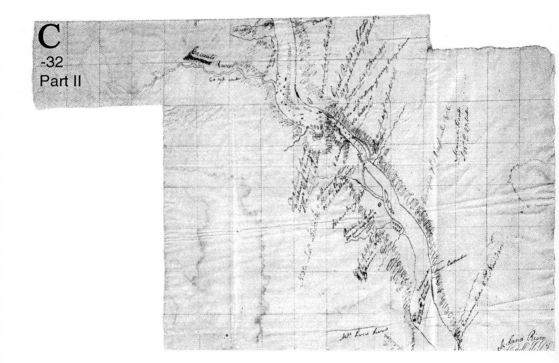

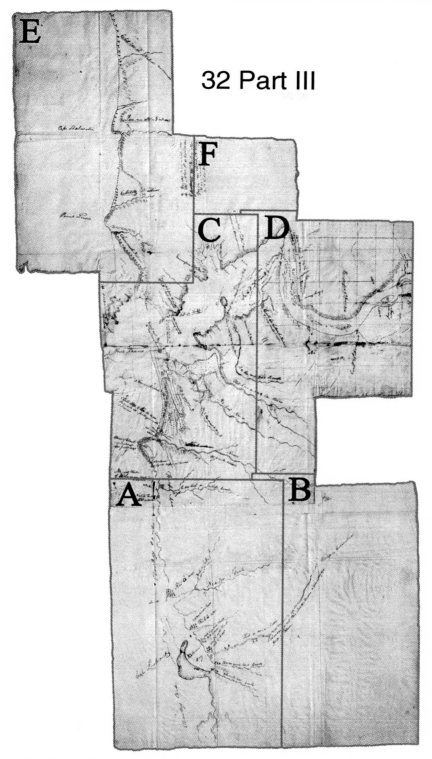

32 Part III

E

F

C D

A B

32. "Sketch of the Columbia River from the forks, & the 19th of October 1805 to the
1st of Jany on the Pacific Ocean." The map also indicates camping
places on the return journey, in April, 1806.
Part III.

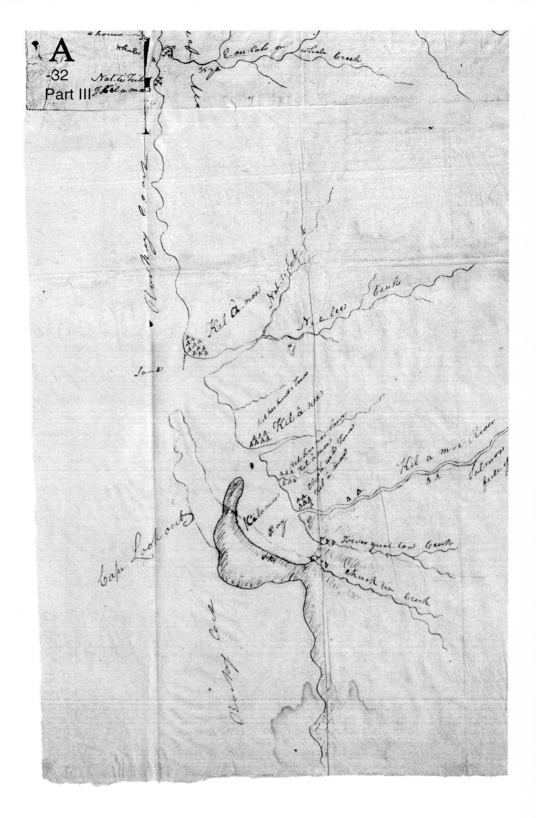

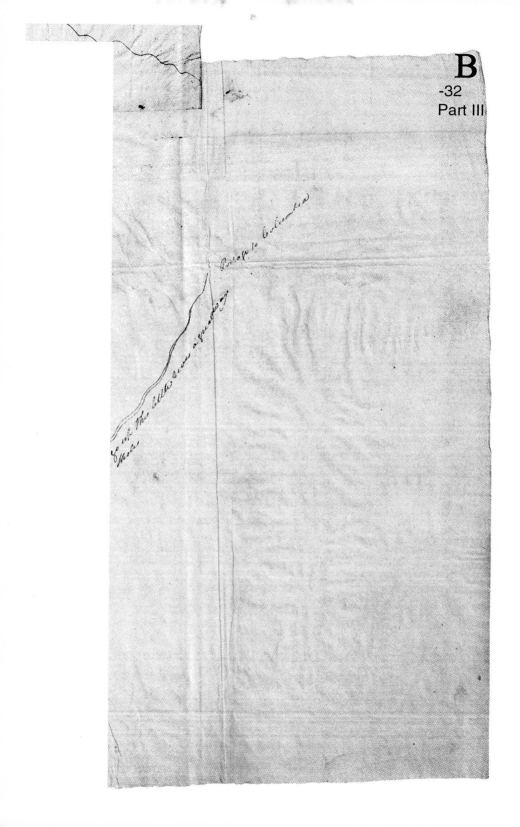

Portage to Columbia

So up the Clk river a ground thro
miles

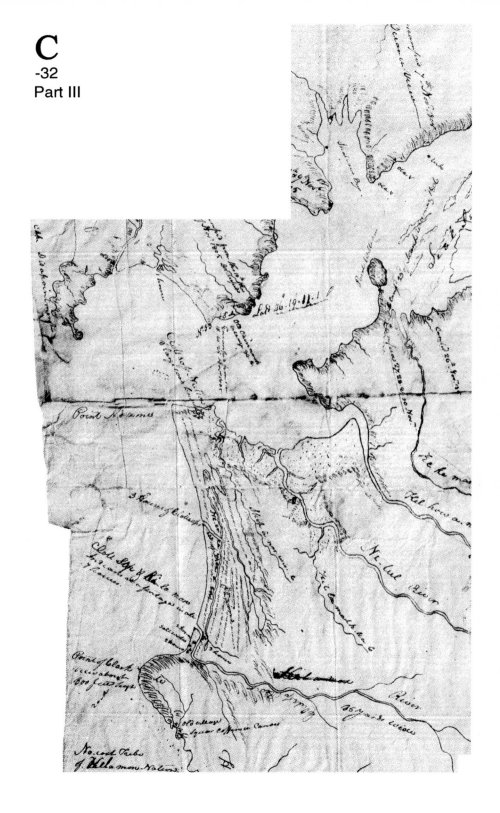

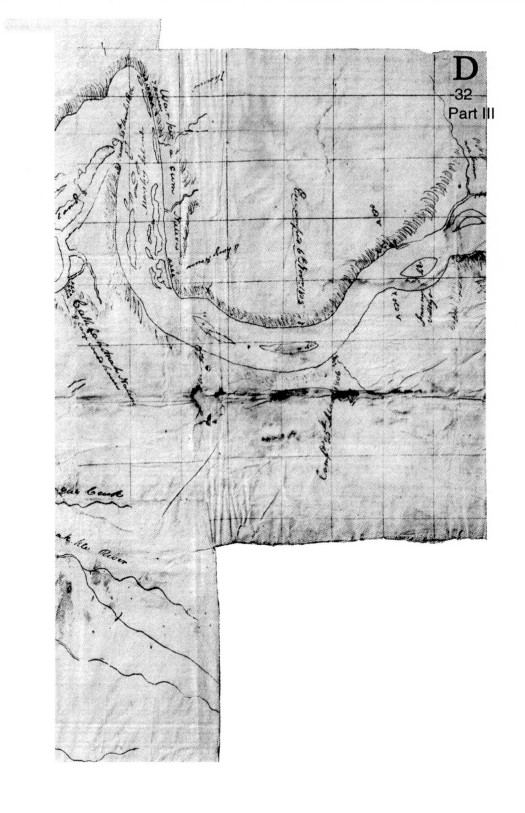

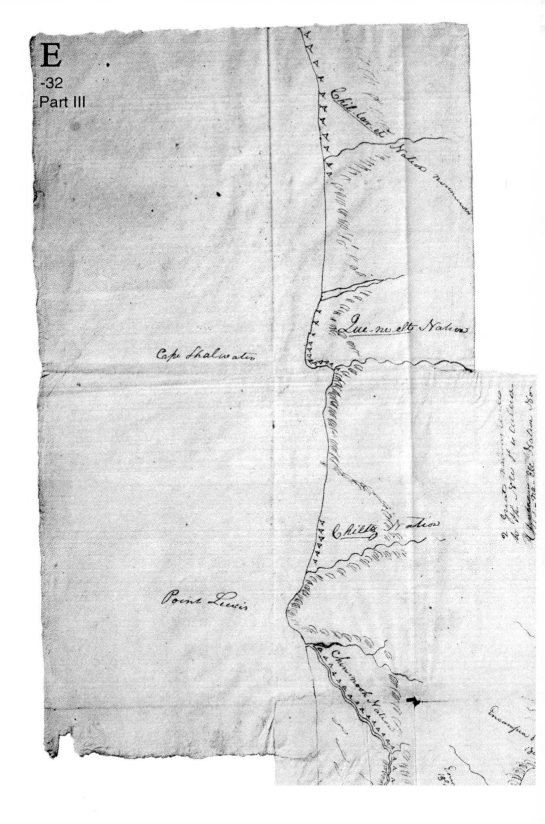

F -32
Part III

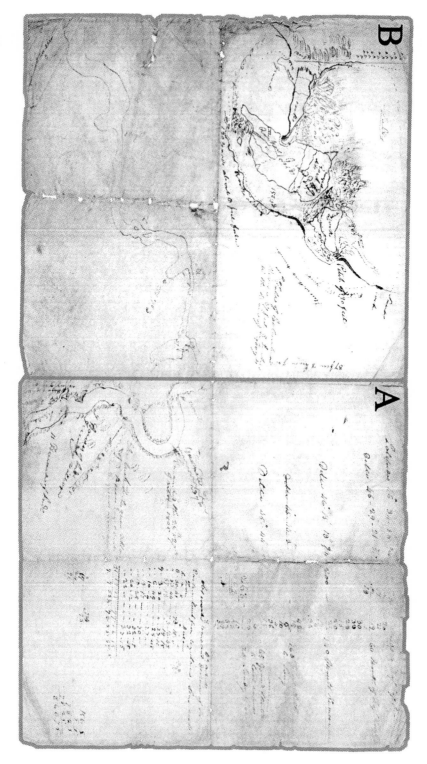

33. Dalles of the Columbia ; with camps of October 26-28, 1805.

A
-33

Latitude 45-34-56

Ditto 46-29-21

Ditto 46° 15' 18"

~~Ditto 45 44 3"~~

Ditto 45° 44'

17	21	
	12	60 Mouth of
73		
	30	
	39	
	23	
	15	
	20	
200		140 Mouth the
	42	
	12	163
	6	6
	70	
	36	
		65
	6	6
263		25
	10	
	32	
	29	

Observed time and Distance of the Eastern limb from

Time				Distance		
h	m	s		°	'	"
8	50	41		73	15	0
"	53	44		73	16	45
"	57	18		"	19	15
9	3	20		"	23	15
"	6	40		"	26	45
"	10	9		"	27	"
"	15	57		"	30	"
"	18	25		"	22	5
"	20	12		"	32	45
"	22	"		"	33	15
4	7	33		73	25	37.5

67	174	150
24	73	
72		7821
		8607

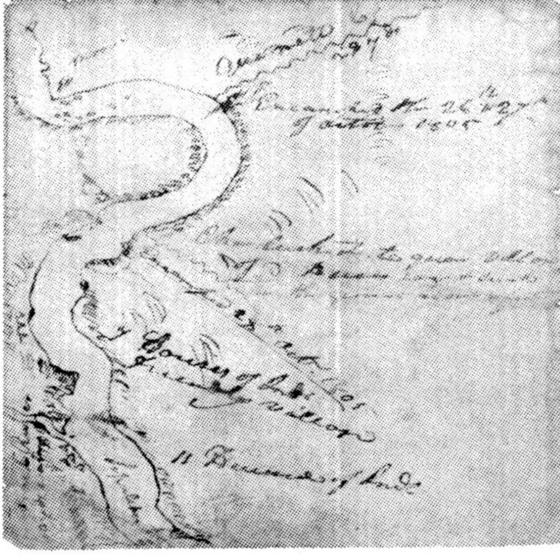

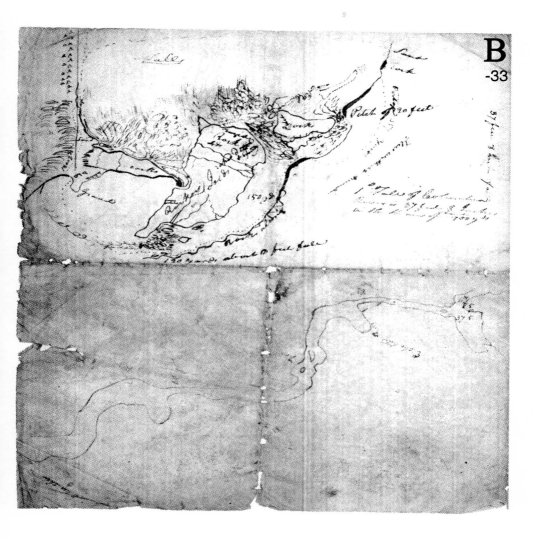

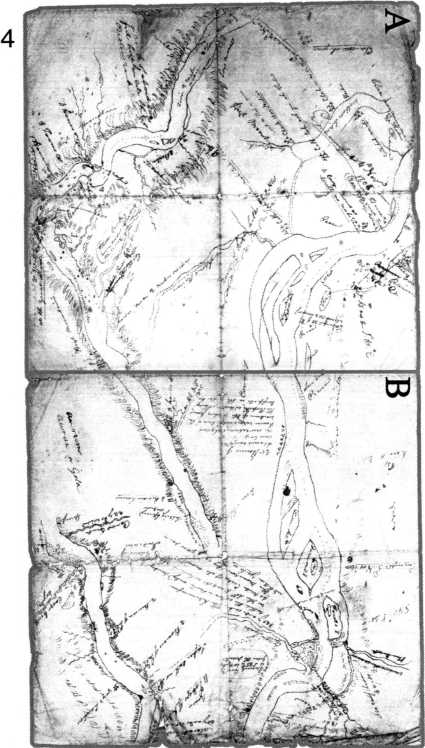

34. The Columbia River, from the Cascades to Wappato Island—showing camps of
November 2-4, 1805, and the return camp on March 30, 1806 ;
also a rough sketch of the Cascades.

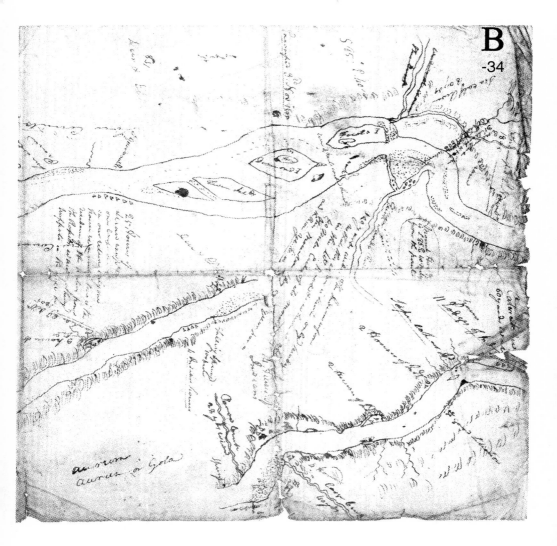

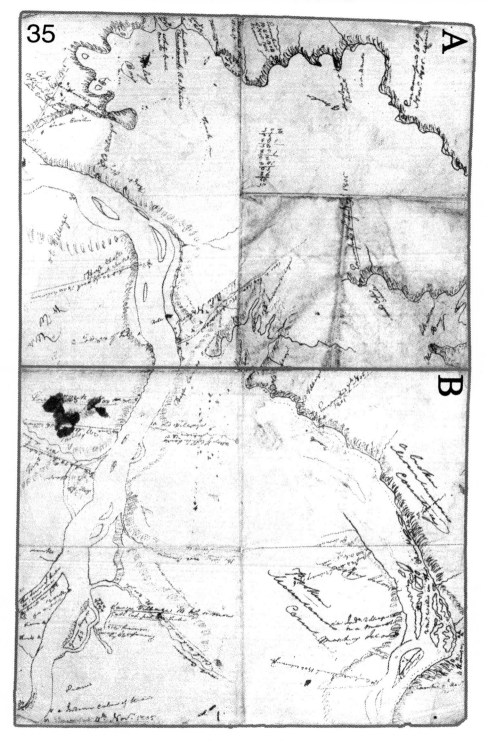

35

A

B

A medley of sketches : { I. Pacific Coast, in neighborhood of Haley's Bay---showing camps of November 8-17, 1805.
{ II. Camps of November 6, 7 ; detail---showing return camps of March 24, 25, 1806.

III. Camp of November 8 ; detail.

IV. Lower reaches of Columbia, Showing outward camps of November 4-6, 1805, and the
return camps of March 26-29, 1806.

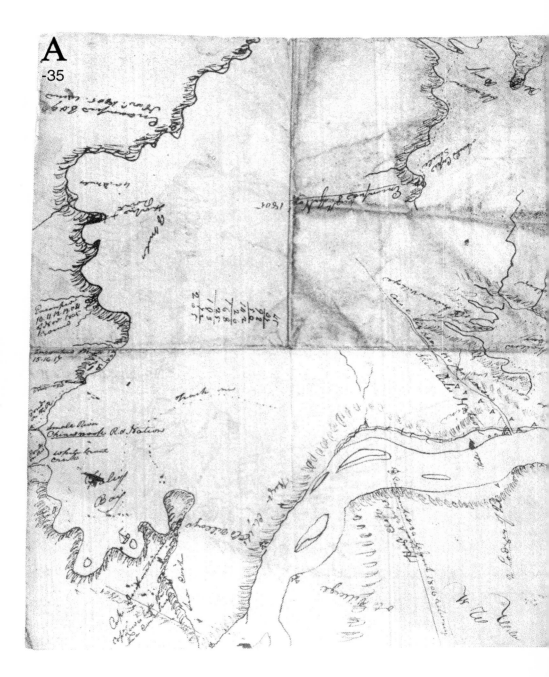

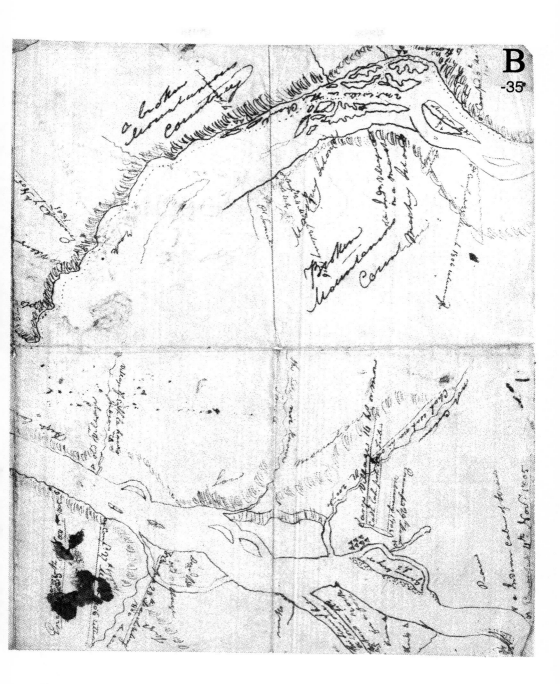

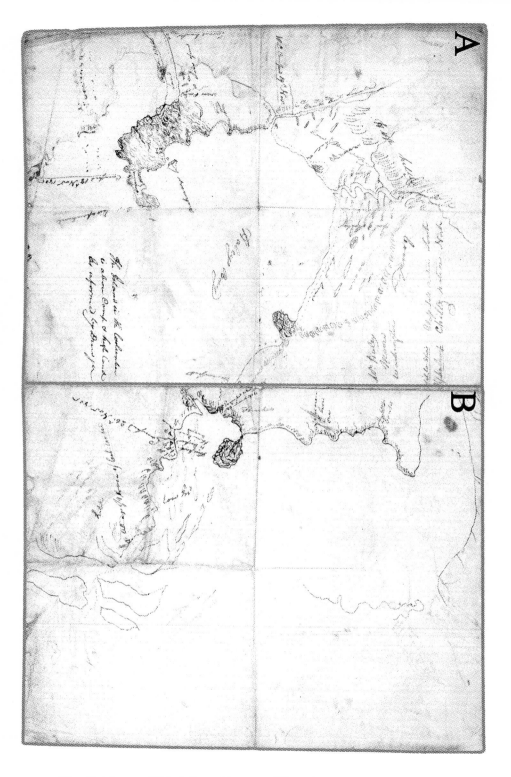

A

B

36.   Sketch map of Haley's Bay, with camps of November 18, 19, and 26, 1805, and
return camp of March 23, 1806.

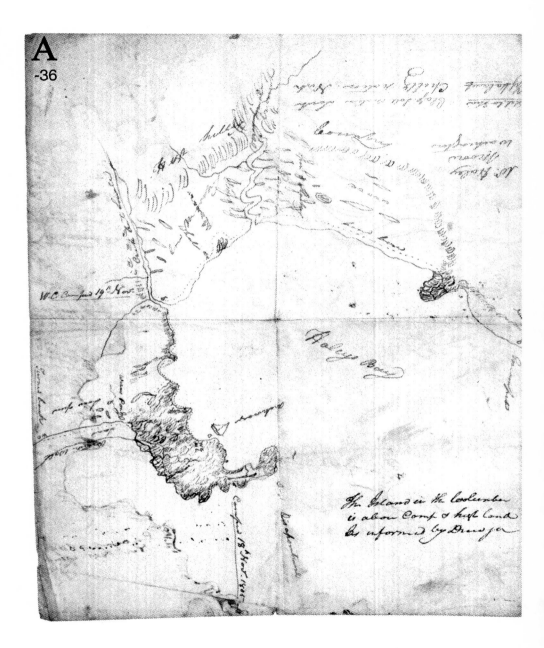

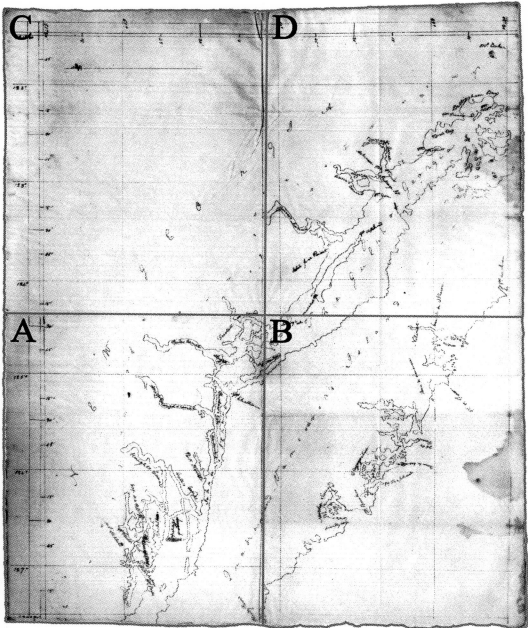

C D

A B

37. Lewis's sketch-map of Vancouver's Island, Nootka Sound, etc.

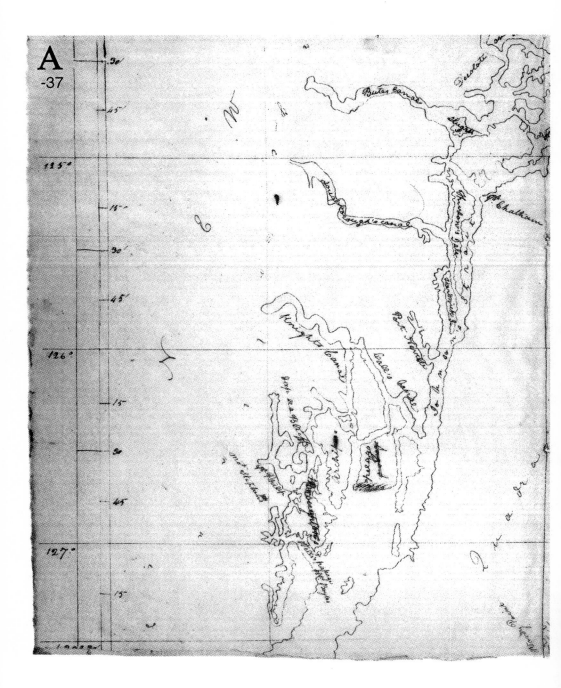

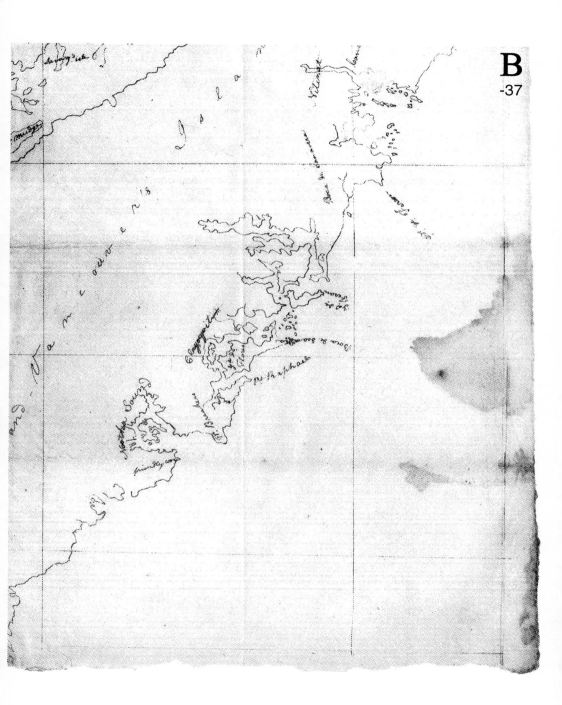

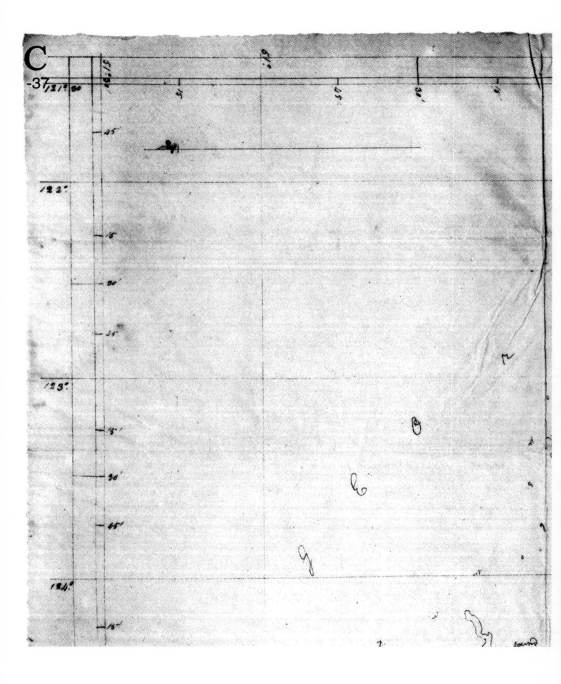

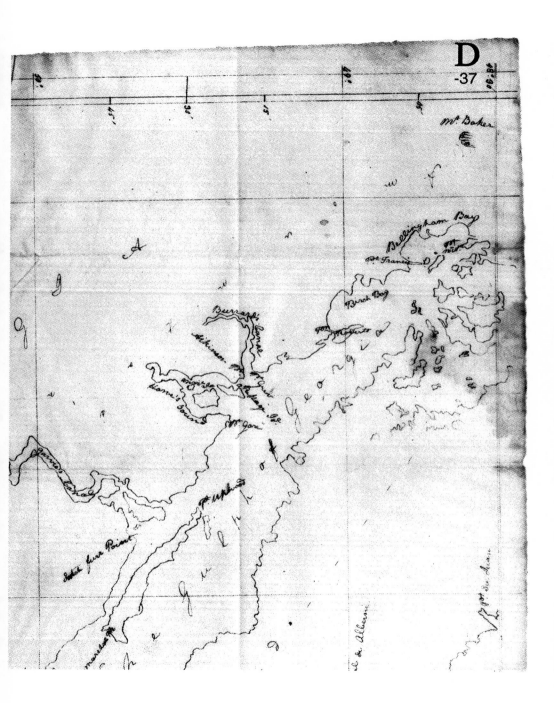

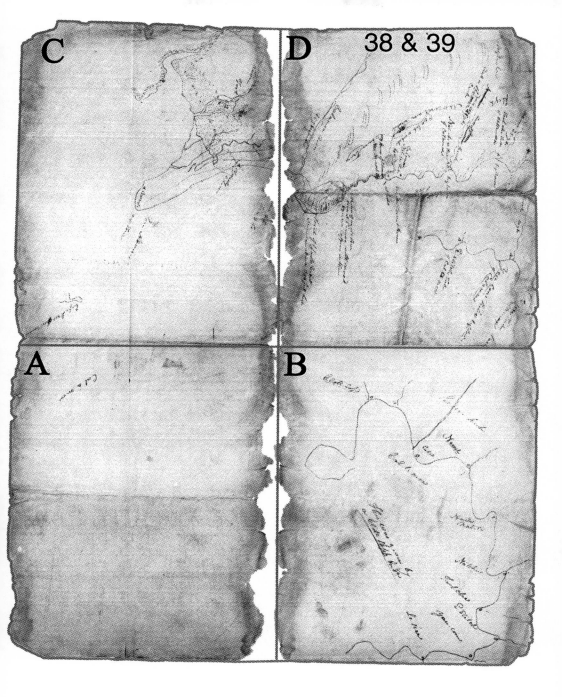

38. Sketch-map of the mouth of Columbia River and Pacific Coast, with the route of Clark, January 6-10, 1806---showing tribes, measurements of streams, and elevations.

39. Sketch-map "given by a Clattsopp Ind[n]," showing the mouth of the Columbia, with adjacent tribes.

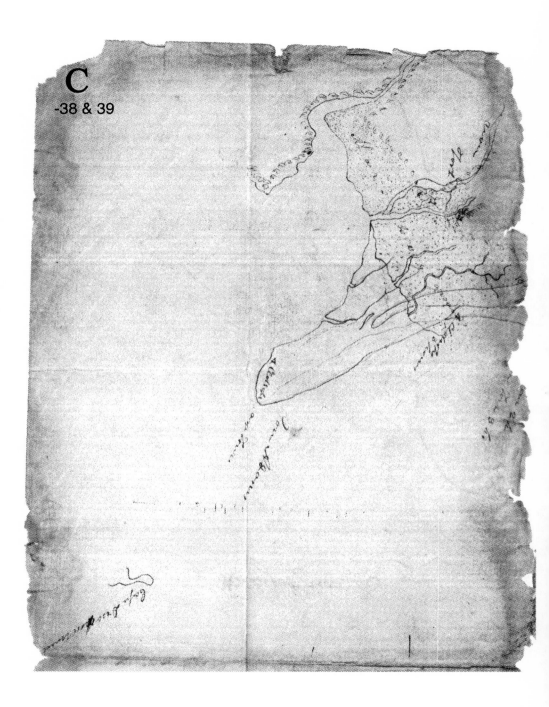

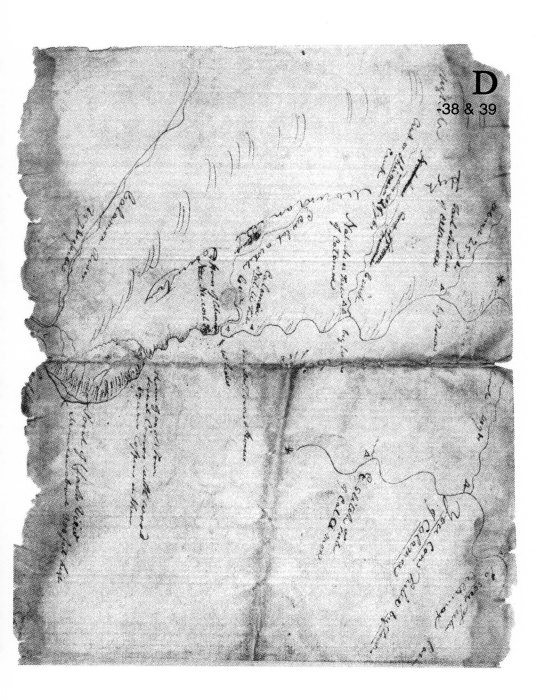

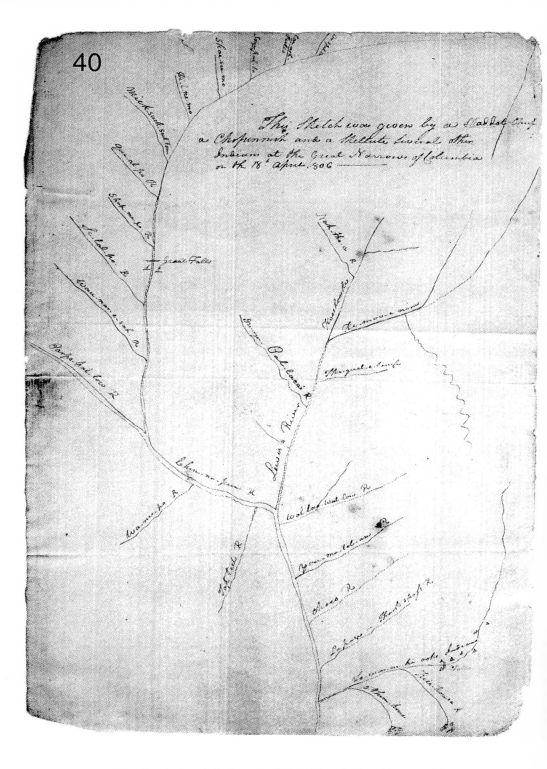

40.   Sketch given by Indians, April 18, 1806, at the Great Narrows of the
Columbia, showing the basin of Lewis's River.

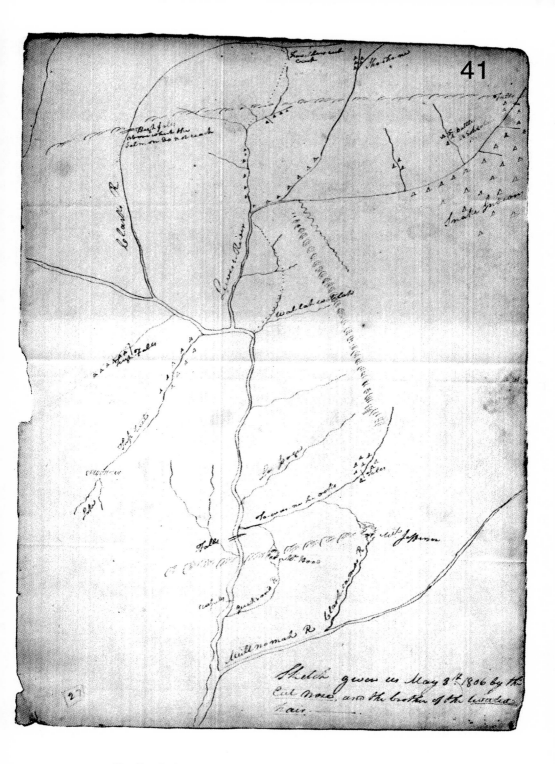

41. Sketch given by Cutnose, etc., May 8, 1806 ; showing Indian trails over the continental divide.

42. Sketch by Hohastillpilp, May 29, 1806, showing Indian trails
over the continental divide.

43. Sketch obtained from Indians at Flathead River camp, May 29-31, 1806. It shows trails and villages from the mouth of Clark's River to the upper Missouri.

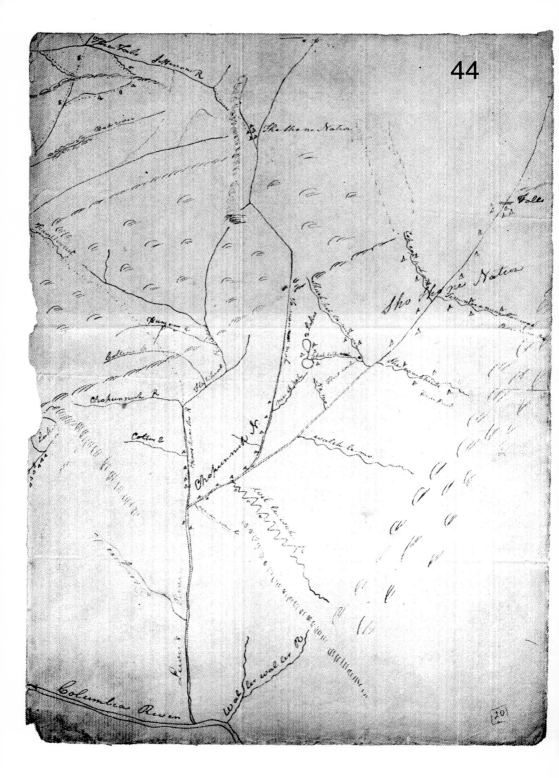

44.   Indian sketch-map of the Lewis River system, showing trails and Indian villages.

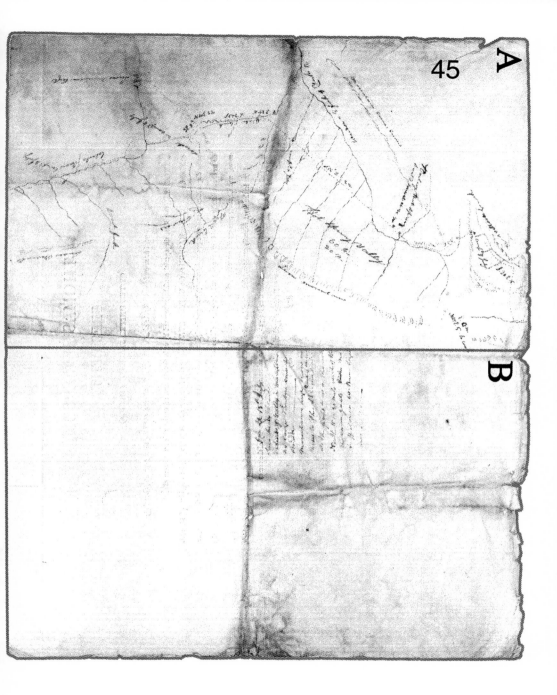

45. Clark's route from Bitterroot River to Forks of Jefferson, showing camping places from July 4-8, 1806.

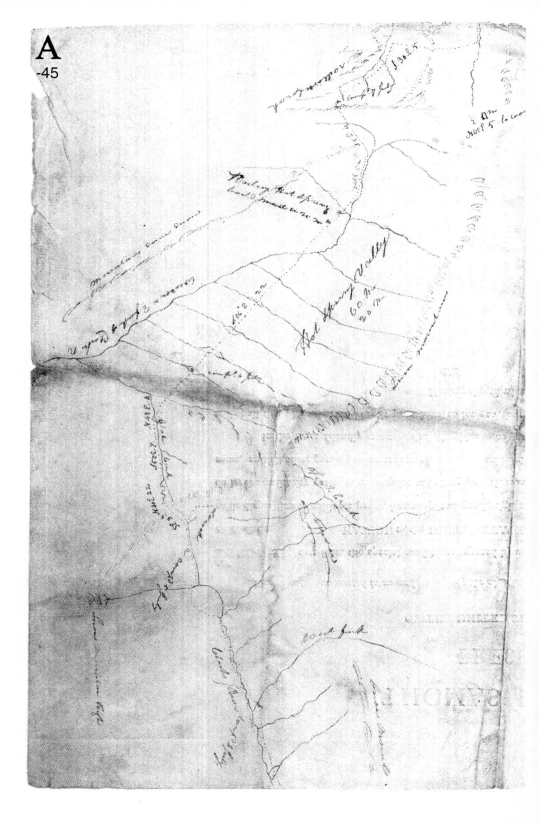

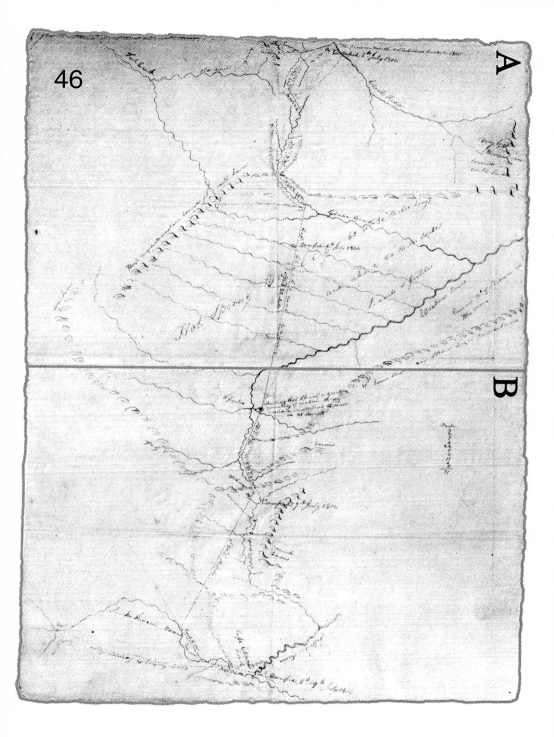

46 "Sketch of Cap͏ Clarks rout from Clark River to the head of Jeffersons River."—July 5-9, 1806.

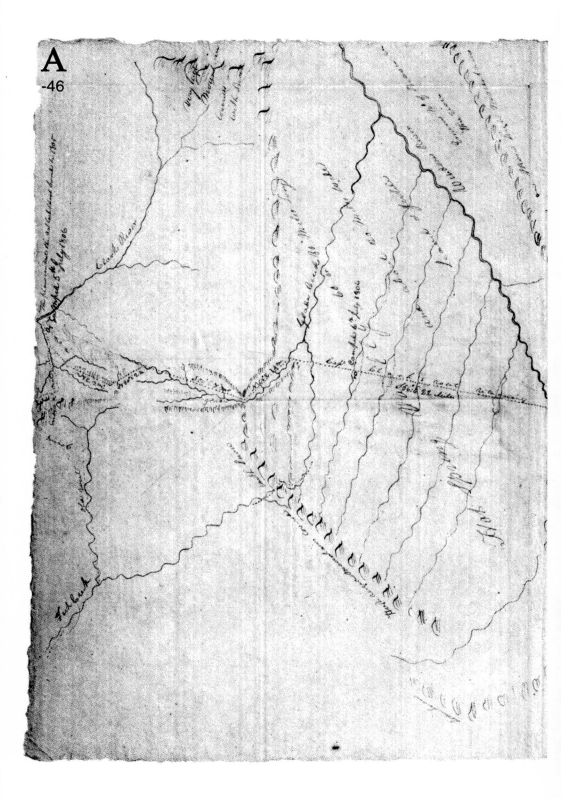

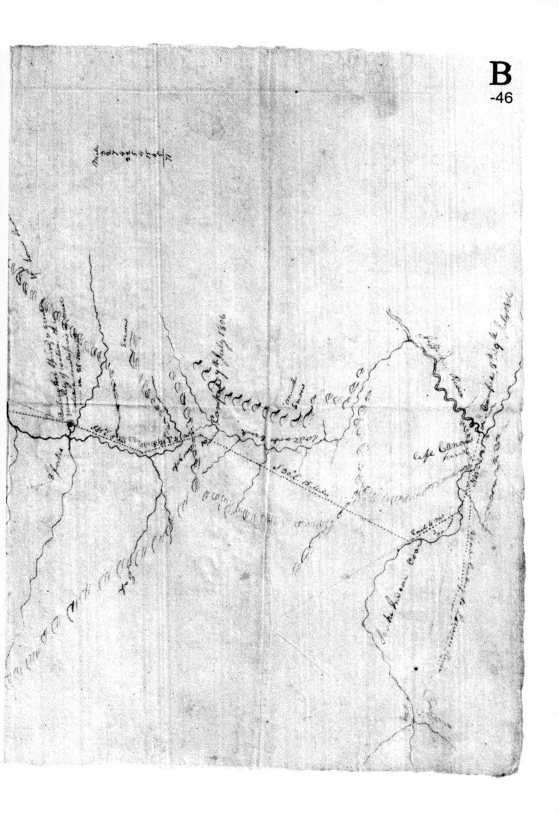

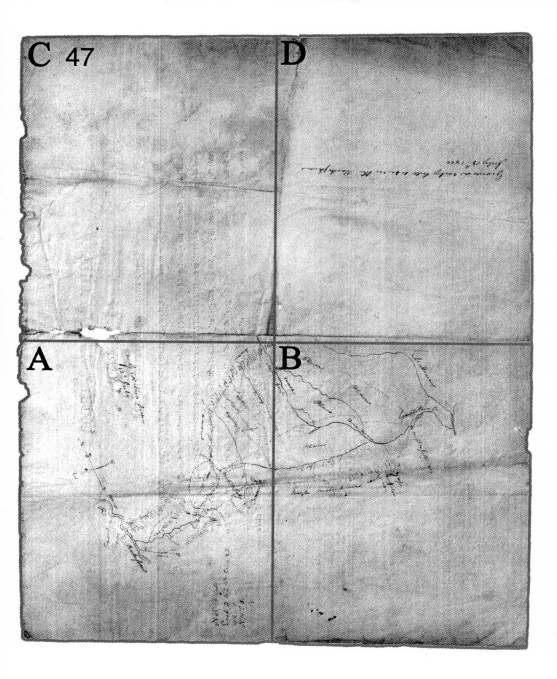

C 47

D

A

B

47. Sketch-map of Gallatin and Madison Rivers, with Clark's trail to the Yellowstone,
July 13, 14, 1806.

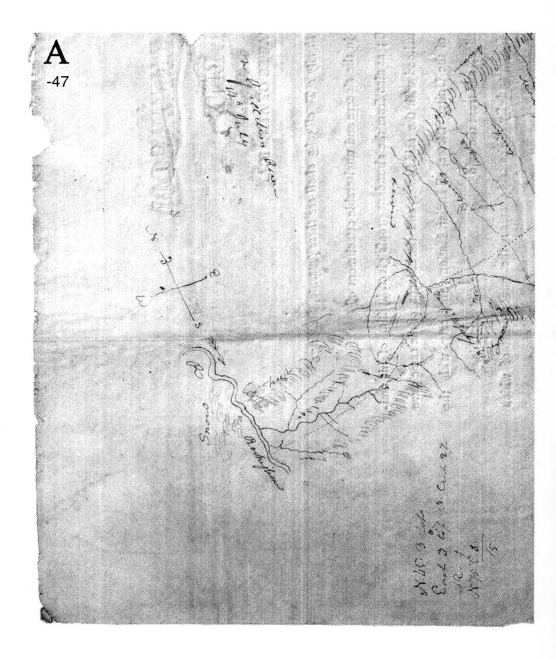

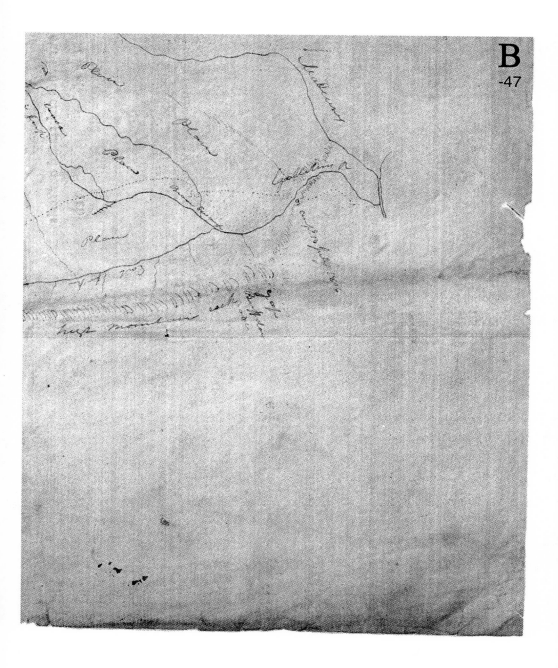

C
-47

Grows in rocky hill sides on the Rockyshwn
July 18ᵗʰ 1806

48

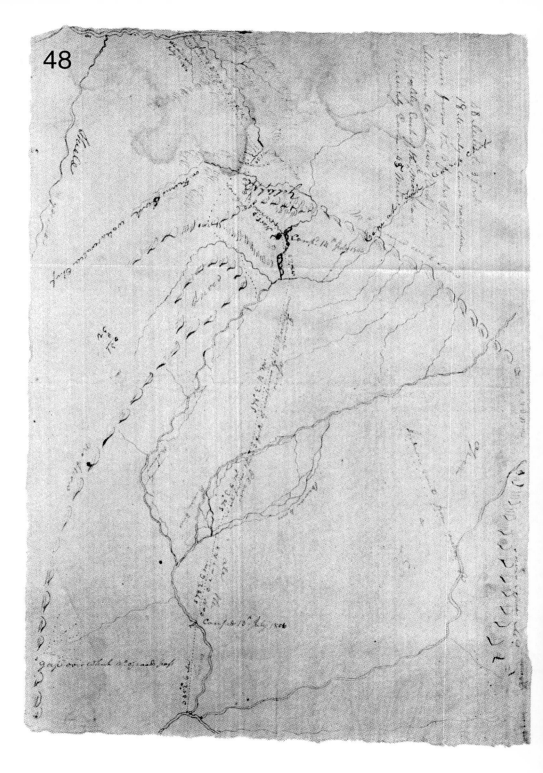

48. Indian trails, derived from native information, of a route from the Three Forks of the
Missouri to the Yellowstone, indicating Clark's camping places of
July 13-15, 1806.

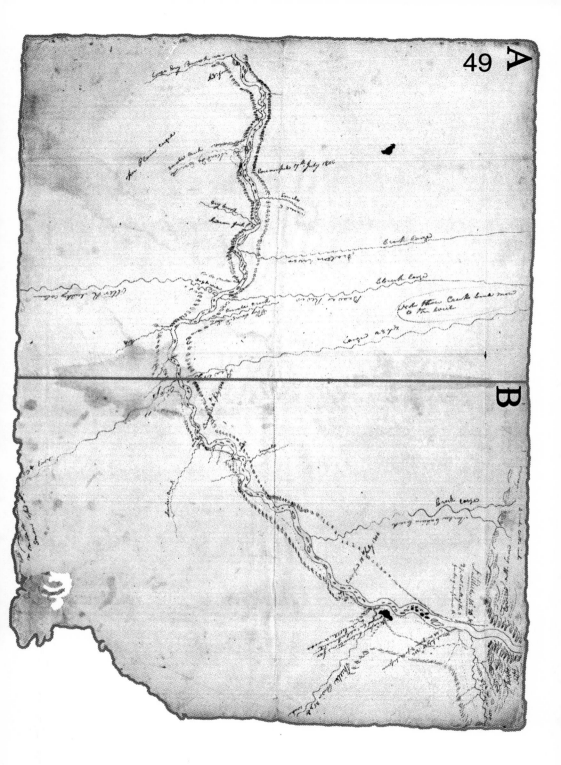

49. The Yellowstone, from the place where Clark reached it to Stillwater Creek, showing Clark's camps, July 15-7 [17], 1806.

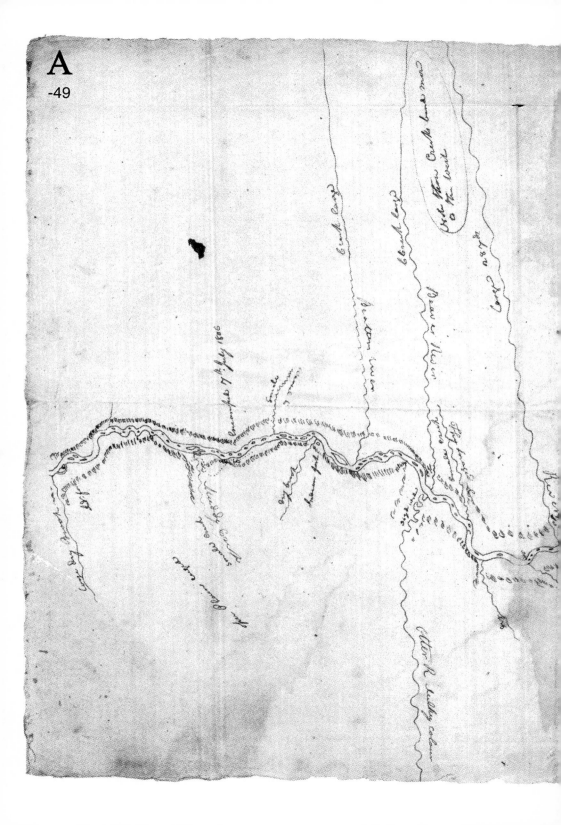

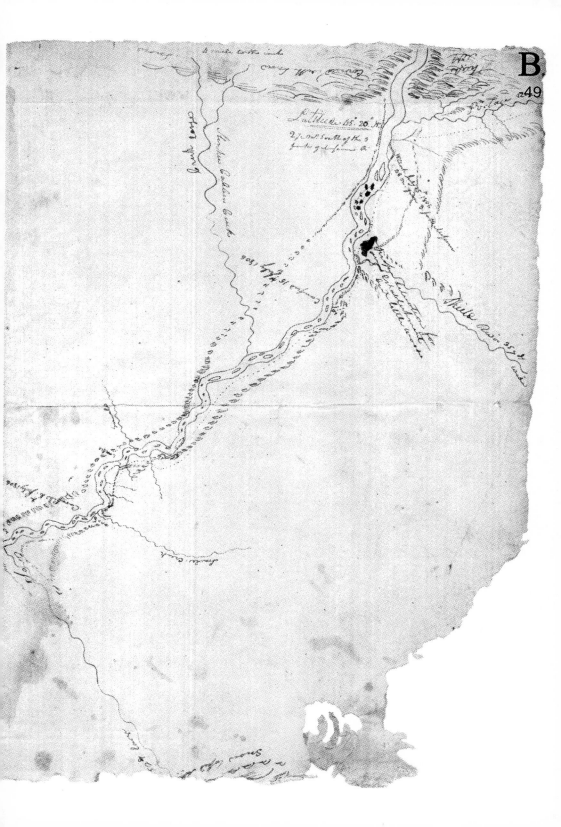

B.
219

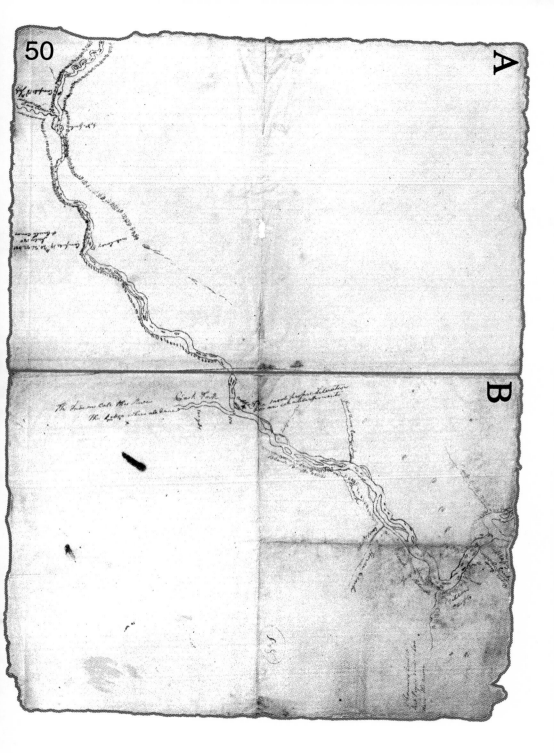

50. The Yellowstone, from Rose [Stillwater] Creek to Pryor's River, July 18-24, 1806, showing the place where Clark's canoes were built.

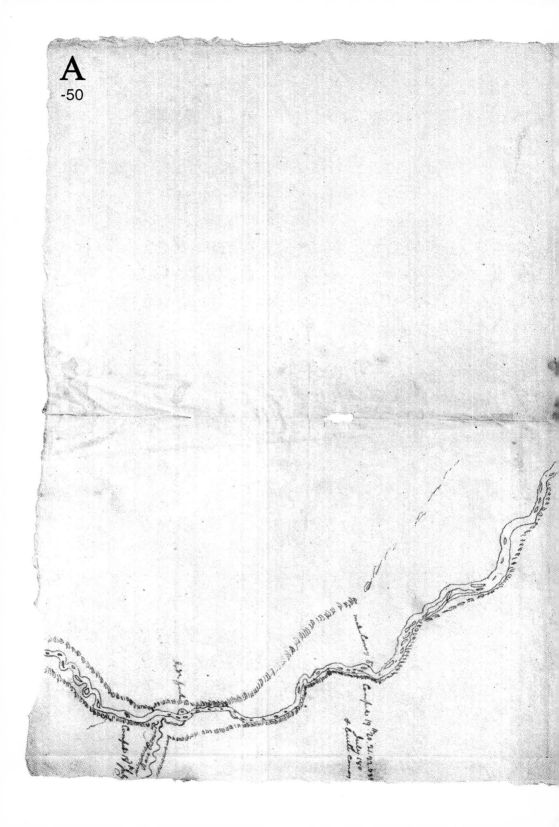

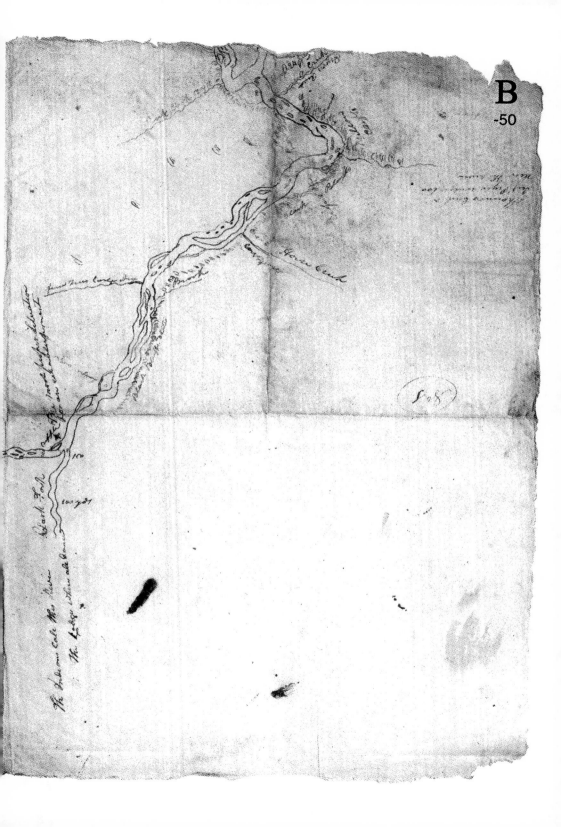

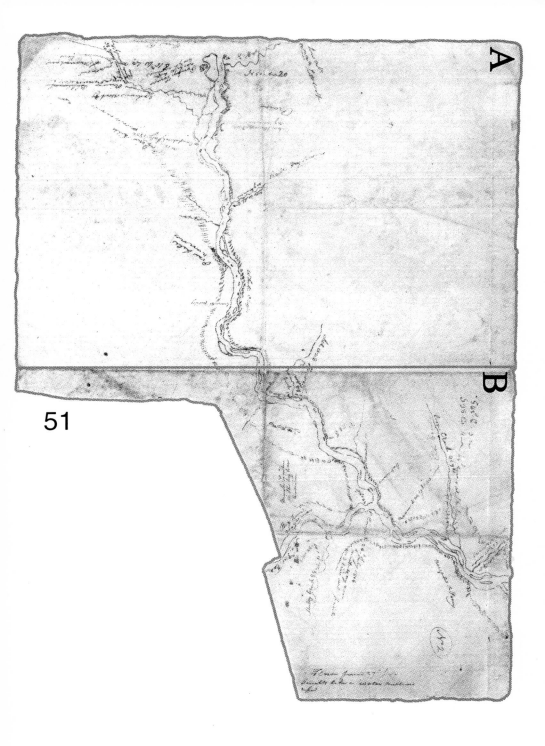

A

B

51

51.   The Yellowstone, from Pompey's Pillar to Little Wolf River (Van Horn Creek),
passing the mouth of Bighorn River, showing Clark's camps, July 25, 26, 1806.

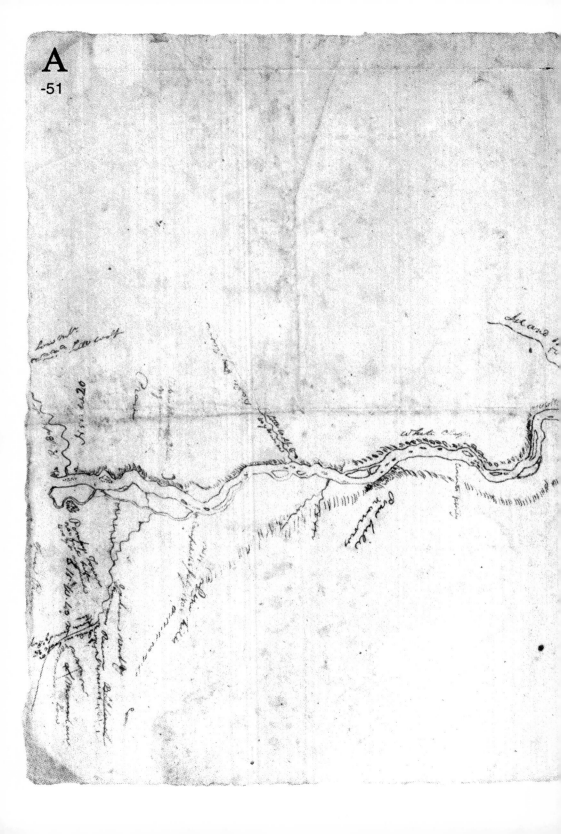

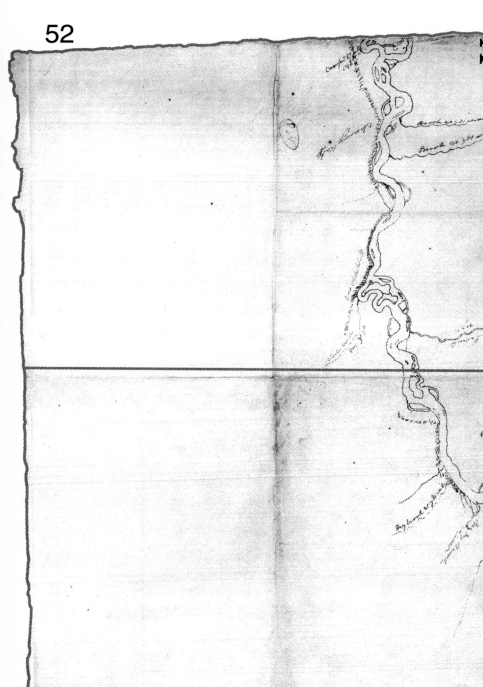

52. The Yellowstone from Van Horn Creek to Camping Place, July 27, 1806.

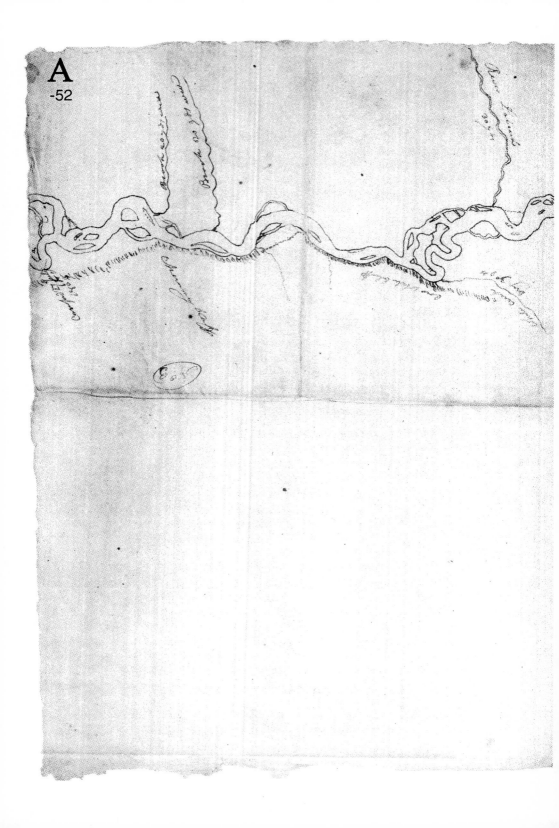

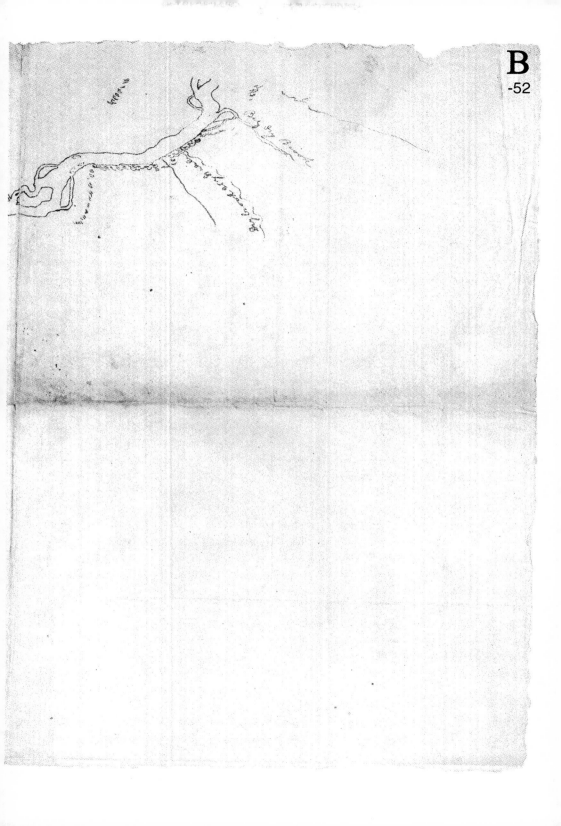

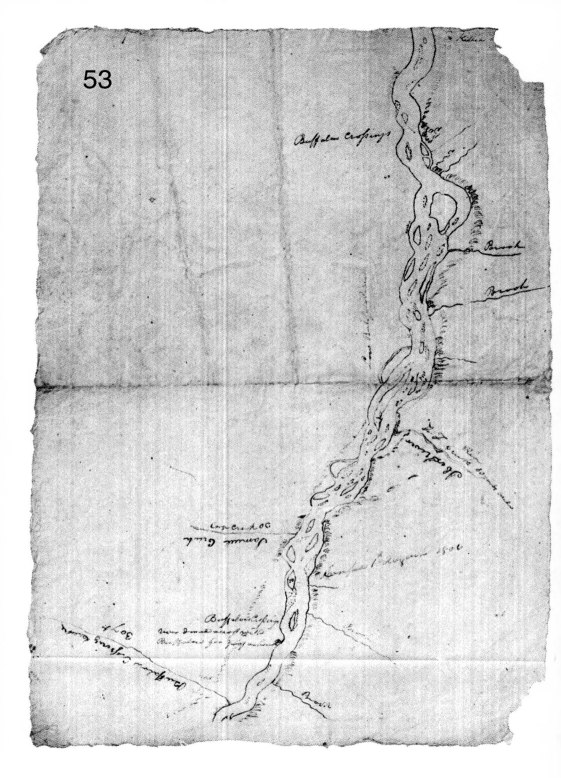

53. The Yellowstone, near its junction with the Missouri, showing Clark's camping place of August 1, 1806 ; also indicating buffalo crossings.

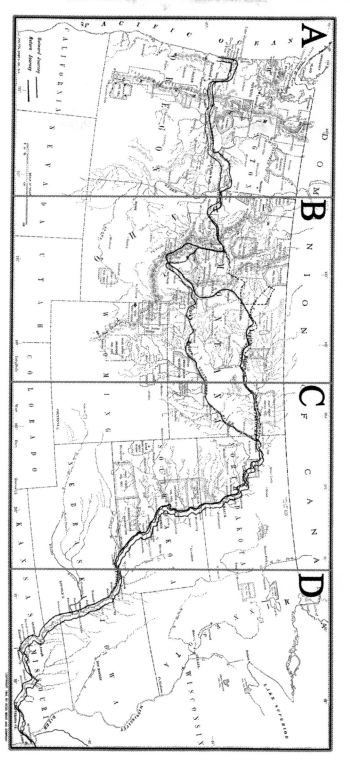

54. Route of the Lewis and Clark Expedition, showing its relation to modern geographical conditions. Drawn expressly for the present publication, and based upon a study of the original manuscript charts herein reproduced in fac-simile.

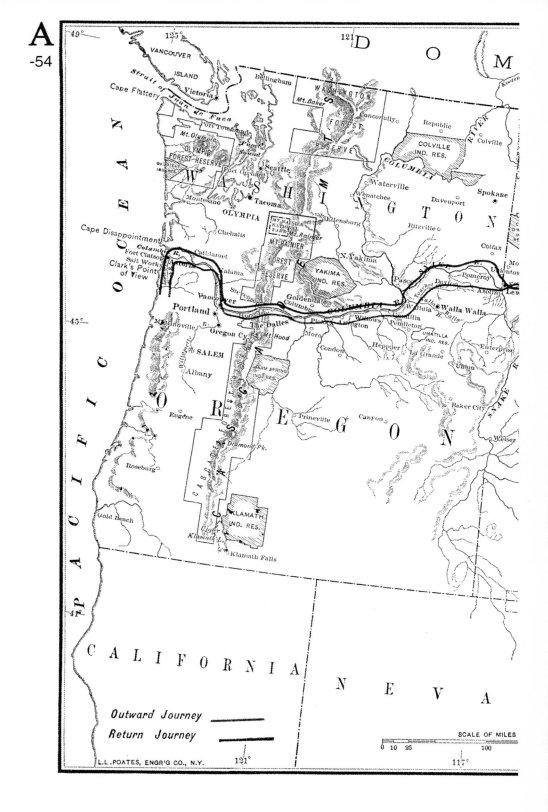

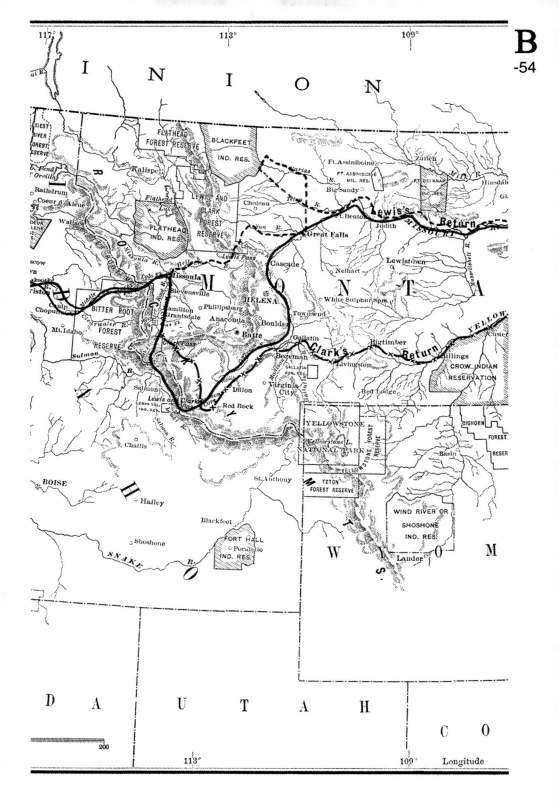

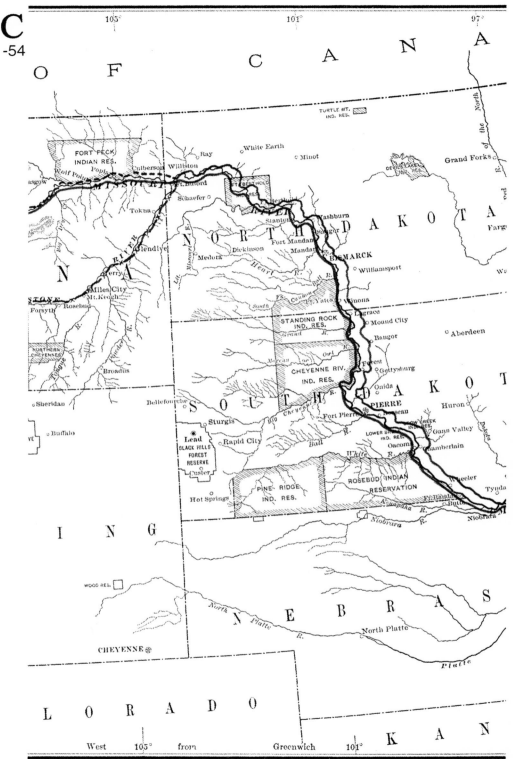

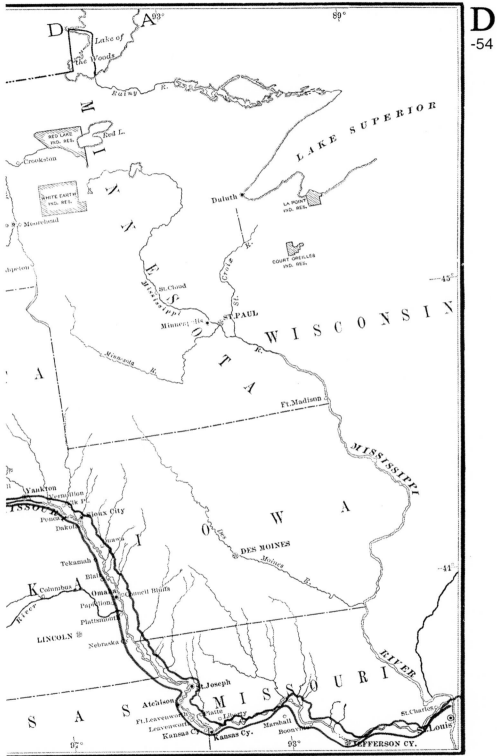

The Original Journals of the Lewis and Clark Expedition

8 Volume Set: Tradepaper ISBN: 158218-651-0   Hardcover ISBN: 1-58218-660-X

Individual Titles:

Volume I Parts 1 & 2
Tradepaper ISBN: 1-58218-652-9   Hardcover ISBN: 1-58218-661-8
Part 1 - Journals and Orderly Book of Lewis and Clark, from River Dubois to the Vermilion River Jan. 30, 1804 - Aug. 24, 1804.
Part 2 - Journals and Order Book of Lewis and Clark, from the Vermilion River to Two-Thousand-Mile Creek Aug. 25, 1804 - May 5, 1805.

Volume II Parts 1 & 2
Tradepaper ISBN: 1-58218-653-7   Hardcover ISBN: 1-58218-662-6
Part 1 - Journals and Orderly Book of Lewis and Clark, from Two -Thousand-Mile Creek to the Great Falls of the Missouri May 6 - June 20, 1805.
Part 2 - Journals and Orderly Book of Lewis and Clark, from the Great Falls of the Missouri to the Shoshoni Camp on Lembi River June 21 - August 20, 1805.

Volume III Parts 1 & 2
Tradepaper ISBN: 1-58218-654-5   Hardcover ISBN: 1-58218-663-4
Part 1 - Journals and Orderly Book of Lewis and Clark, from the Shoshoni Camp on Lembi River to the Encampment on the Columbia River near the Mouth of the Umatilla River.
August 21, 1805 - October 20, 1805.
Part 2 - Journals and Orderly Book of Lewis and Clark, from the Encampment on the Columbia River near the Mouth of the Umatilla River to Fort Clatsop October 21, 1805 - January 20, 1806.

Volume IV Parts 1 & 2
Tradepaper ISBN: 1-58218-655-3   Hardcover ISBN: 1-58218-664-2
Part 1 - Journals and Orderly Book of Lewis and Clark, from Fort Clatsop (preparation for the start home) to Fort Clatsop, January 21 - May 17, 1806.
Part 2 - Journals and Orderly Book of Lewis and Clark, from Fort Clatsop (preparation for the start home) to Musquetoe Creek March 18 - May 7, 1806.

Volume V Parts 1 & 2
Tradepaper ISBN 1-58218-656-1   Hardcover ISBN: 1-58218-665-0
Part 1 - Journals of Lewis and Clark, from Musquetoe Creek to Travellers Rest.
May 8 - July 2, 1806.
Part 2 - Journals of Lewis and Clark, from Travellers Rest to St. Louis.
July 3 - September 26, 1806.

Volume VI Parts 1 & 2
Tradepaper ISBN: 1-58218-657-X   Hardcover ISBN: 1-58218-666-9
Part 1 - Scientific Data accompanying the Journals of Lewis and Clark; Geography, Ethnology, Zoology.
Part 2 - Botany, Mineralogy, Meteorology, Astronomy, and Miscellaneous Memoranda.

Volume VII Parts 1 & 2
Tradepaper ISBN: 1-58218-658-8   Hardcover ISBN: 1-58218-667-7
Part 1 - Journals of Charles Floyd and Joseph Whitehouse; Appendix.
Part 2 - Appendix; Index.

Atlas -Tradepaper ISBN: 1-58218-659-6   Hardcover ISBN: 1-58218-668-5

CPSIA information can be obtained at www.ICGtesting.com
Printed in the USA
BVOW030714050312

284388BV00002B/26/A